Things I Never Told My Children: My Story of Life, Love, Luck, Laughter and Loss

BY

Jeanne Poett Leonard

Azalea Art Press
Sonoma | CA

ISBN: 978-1-943471-34-8

Cover Painting | Jeanne Poett Leonard
2017

For Andrew & Cynthia

and

For My Friends

**Friendship is the hardest thing in the world
to explain. It's not something you learn in school.
But if you haven't learned the meaning of friendship,
you really haven't learned anything.**

- Muhammed Ali

I truly believe that people don't come into our lives by
accident. I regret not being able to include each one of
you in my story and the many unforgettable memories
you have and still provide to make my life complete.
I am forever grateful to you and know how fortunate I am
to have such giving, thoughtful people in my life.
You are family to me.

Foreword

These pages tell my story, a collection of memories of past events as I remember them. The names are real and the details are as true as I remember them.

Any inaccuracies regarding dates or facts are mine. It is not meant to be a historical account, but simply a revival of some of my most unforgettable times, places and people, so many who are no longer with us.

My hope is that I haven't offended or embarrassed anyone in the telling of my story.

- Jeanne Poett Leonard
August 2018

The Beginning
1942

I was born in Pasadena, California and lived there until I was eight months old. I grew up in a town called Hillsborough, a suburb 30 miles south of San Francisco (though no one would dare to call it suburbia). From early on it was known to be a rather grand place to live, though I never thought of it as different from any other small town, and my immediate family could hardly have been known as "grand."

It sounds as if our forebears were rather fancy but we were not. My great-grandparents on my father's side were among the founders of the community in the early 1900s and their family was responsible for naming many of the roads in Hillsborough (i.e. Poett Road, Carolan Avenue) and the founding of the Burlingame Country Club. They built stately houses wherever they chose, including the Carolands mansion, built in 1914 by my great uncle Frank Carolan and his wife, Harriet Pullman Carolan.

250 Roblar

When we moved from Pasadena, we lived with my father's mother until we found a house of our own which was far from stately! It started out as a perfectly nice house, situated on a tree-lined avenue (there were no streets in Hillsborough—only Lanes, Avenues, Places, Circles,

Boulevards and Terraces). Our house was average for that particular neighborhood and certainly adequate for my parents, my brother, my sister and me . . . and our animals.

250 Roblar

The house at 250 Roblar developed a personality of its own. My father had always had a dog as a child, so there was never a time in my young life when we didn't have dogs, at least one stray of questionable variety, often more than one. Our most unforgettable stray was a mutt we named "Bubbles," who we found wandering the streets of Hillsborough. She had an alluring personality, a face to match and four snow-white socks. I took her everywhere, including to school, in the basket of my bicycle. She adapted well to our family and she and one of our cats, "Blossom," the typically distinctive "orange cat," (a breed unlike any other) became inseparable. They would play together for hours, Blossom screeching with delight as Bubbles grabbed her by the ear or the nape of the neck, pulling her around the house. People would come from miles away just to be entertained by them.

But Bubbles was a wanderer and it became clear that she had come from "the wrong side of the tracks," (my mother's term), as she would repeatedly stray in that direction. We would get regular calls from strangers telling us that she had wandered into their house uninvited. My mother, with a finder's reward in hand, would brave the trip to retrieve Bubbles only to have to repeat the deed again a few days later. Then one day, Bubbles disappeared never to be seen again. We were all distraught, as she had become such a vital member of our family circus. And poor Blossom missed her more than we did.

We always had at least a cat or two. One in particular, a long-haired calico named "Chee-wee," proved to be very prolific and typically produced two litters a year. She chose cozy, safe places to give birth, like under the covers in my brother's bed, and in his sock drawer, which was puzzling as he was the only member of the family who claimed he hated cats. (In those days, it was uncool for a young man to like cats.) The litter that none of us, including Chee-wee, had prepared for, arrived in the back seat of our "Ice Green" '49 Chevrolet en route to Tahoe. Never did she produce fewer than five kittens per litter and this time there were eight!

We never had a problem finding homes for her

kittens and often kept a few to add to our menagerie. My mother had always had "pretty things"— her mother was French, with beautiful taste and style which she passed on to my mother, the favored child. There were lace-trimmed blanket covers on my parents' bed, but the dainty linens never stayed white for long. The dogs ruled the roost and their muddy footprints adorned the bedding more often than not. My mother gave up on any attempt to change my father's leniency towards his beloved animals and decided that nothing so mundane as clean linens or carpets mattered anymore.

My mother's "I-could-care-less" attitude began to take over and it showed throughout the house. Our staircase, which originally had a nice bannister with carefully spaced spindles, had been destroyed during our unsupervised let's-ride-down-the-bannister trips. Rather than restore the staircase, my mother hired a man named Charles to cover the posts with large sheets of plywood and paint them the same pea-soup green that covered the walls of the ladies' restroom at the Shell gas station in downtown San Mateo. This was the color she chose to paint the rest of the house as well. In order to paint the living room, five layers of vintage wallpaper had to be removed layer by layer. We were all required to help, a task that took forever, as the only tools we had to work with were flimsy painters' spatulas. As we chiseled away, we were given strict warnings not to gouge the underlying layer of plaster that awaited the coat of green. Even the frame on the portrait of the Virgin Mary and Baby Jesus that hung over the

4

fireplace was painted that deadly green.

The only other time we were all in the living room together as a family, aside from Christmas morning, was when my father came home from duck hunting. We were all invited to join him in plucking every feather out of the poor dead birds that he plopped down on the living room rug. We put a layer of newspaper down but that didn't prevent the feathers from flying around the living room, attaching themselves to the rugs, the furniture, the windows and, of course, to us. We had feathers everywhere—on our clothes, up our noses, in our hair, and they were not easy to un-stick once they had landed. The naked carcasses lying before us, we dutifully earned our coveted duck dinner all the while covered in feathers.

This house at 250 Roblar became the center of activity for the neighborhood and in later years became known as "Ma Poett's Boarding House." My friends couldn't wait to come to our house because whatever we wanted to do, we were allowed to do. Nothing was out of bounds. This included painting our bedrooms any color at any time, moving the furniture around whichever way we wanted it and even exchanging bedrooms, which meant moving mattresses, beds and dressers out into the hall, over the stairs and into our respective new rooms. This was done, as usual, without parental supervision.

It seems that my parents were rarely there. They had a brisk social schedule, so any overseeing came from the lucky housekeeper-of-the-moment. My mother had a good friend who moved to New York and would stay with us when she visited California. She was never quite sure if she'd be able to make it up to her room, as more often than not there was a mattress or dresser blocking the stairs. It seems we were in the process of either trading rooms or painting them every time she came to visit. Ours really was a life every kid dreams about—few rules or attempts at order. As a result, I developed a need for order and for detail in my later life.

Carolan & Harry
250 Roblar, 1945

Gammy

My father's mother, "Gammy," was a lovely, refined, gentle woman. To this day I regret not having known her better as we were growing up. She lived just around the corner from us in an impressive ivy-covered brown-shingled house. It had an inviting wisteria-draped porch with green wicker furniture and a matching swing that hung from the beams, a perfectly manicured lawn, a bountiful garden of fruit trees and rows of flowers of every kind, numerous servants and a gardener who lived over the garage. Even now, the scents of sweet peas and miniature tea roses remind me of Gammy.

Gammy & Me, 1942

Though slight in stature, she was the model matriarch, never raising her voice, and from my view, seemed as if she found everybody and everything "cunning" or "becoming," words I've not heard since Gammy died. We had regular Sunday night dinners at her perfectly set table with an immaculate white tablecloth, five pieces of silverware, three plates, three crystal glasses, a finger bowl and a little silver dish filled with mixed nuts at each place. It was there that we learned how to behave at the table and how to serve ourselves from large silver platters passed by a uniformed butler.

The dinners were always amazing. One soup that I can still taste was a thick, very rich curry/crab bisque which I am certain has never been duplicated, anywhere. At Thanksgiving and at Christmas we had the usual traditional fare—turkey, dressing, mashed potatoes, creamed onions, green beans, mincemeat pie—but there was nothing usual about it. It was done and served to perfection. Only on these two occasions did the silver temple adorned with angels, a museum piece really, stand at the center of the long table. Gammy's dinners were our only opportunities to connect with our cousins, aunts and uncles and an old maid aunt who smelled funny and who every week succeeded in stirring up political arguments between even the most uninformed among us.

Unfortunately, I never knew my grandfather, as he died before I was born.

Grand-mere

My maternal grandmother was half French and was known to us as "Grand-mere." She was about as down-to-earth as anyone could be, maybe because she had married a rancher and lived in Brentwood, the boonies to us, where they grew apricots, raspberries, tomatoes, figs, and all kinds of vegetables. She drove a tractor when extra help was needed, a pick-up truck and a 1943 Ford convertible. The ranch may have been "out there" but she succeeded in maintaining a charming, warm Victorian house there, with a wraparound screened porch, beautiful antique furniture and fine rugs that had been passed down through her family. She never lost her inborn "chic."

We would visit her and Grandpa on the ranch for several days at a time and each time we were there, Grandmere would bring out "Eloise at the Plaza," and "Madeline," the charming book about the 12 French schoolgirls. We always had a good time until she made us drink warm milk at bedtime, which was 7:00 pm on the dot. Not only was it much too early and still daylight, but the warm milk, with its sickening thick membrane floating on top, made me gag. I never liked milk at any temperature, even as a young child, but she had little sympathy for that, as all children were supposed to like milk, and I had to force it down.

We spent much of our time with the two children of the ranch foreman who were about our age. They were aware of my grandmother's unconscionable bedtime policy and they agreed to help make it a little more bearable for us. After we were supposedly tucked in, they would appear below our bedroom window with a homemade walkie-talkie, which worked well enough, and baskets of popcorn we hoisted up with a simple string arrangement. They kept us entertained until 8:00 or 8:30, a reasonable time for them to head home and for us to think about going to sleep.

When Grandpa died, Grand-mere moved to an apartment in San Mateo, a mile from our house. At one point she tried to teach a group of us, my sister's and my friends, aged 8-10 years, her language. We learned a few words and most of the Lord's Prayer, but we were far more interested in the sugary, pastel petit-fours she brought with her than learning French. What a waste of a perfect opportunity for all of us. I am now, at age 76, taking a beginning French course, finding it *trés difficile* and wishing every day that I had taken advantage of Grand-mere's willingness to teach us way back then.

Aunt Eliza

Then there was our Aunt Eliza. She was our mother's aunt, married to Grand-mere's brother, Uncle John. We barely knew her when we were young. In fact, on the rare occasions when we did see them, they had just arrived from their summer stay in Europe, en route to their house in Palm Springs. They seemed so chic, so unapproachable. Eliza always wore a hat and the one I remember the most was a pink velvet beret with huge jewels surrounding its rim. They never had children of their own. They worshipped my mother, the beautiful one, and paid no attention to her two siblings.

Aunt Eliza by Unknown Artist

After Uncle John died, Eliza rented an apartment in San Francisco or Marin every summer. We visited her at her summer locations, learned then of her impish ways and named her "Eloise," (after the devilish little girl who lived at the Plaza), which she considered the utmost compliment. But it wasn't until after my mother died that I got to really know Eliza, as she took me under her wing just as she had my mother. She took me shopping at only the most exclusive stores in San Francisco, where she considered most of the sales people "perfect asses," and didn't hide her sentiments. We "lunched" at the Town and Country Club where everyone knew her and treated her as if she were royalty. I visited her often in Palm Springs. Her charming and stylish country French house was the only one like it in the desert. She had dinner parties almost every night and her guests were never dull—there were actors, gossip columnists, vintners and designers. She charmed them all.

11

In the late 1980s Mike Wallace interviewed her for a segment on "Sixty Minutes" as the the Grand Dame of Palm Springs. That she was! She died at the age of 99, a character to the end.

Mom

My mother was a natural-born beauty, which was to her advantage throughout her life, though she did have a sparkling personality as well. People flocked to her as she was a good listener, a good friend, and had, unquestionably, the gift of gab. She was the eldest and favorite of three children. She attended convent schools and easily absorbed the rules of etiquette taught by the nuns, which was more important than academics in those days. She and my father were often on the go so I don't have those memories of the warm fuzzy hugs from my mother that some of my friends hold of their mothers, but I do remember how great she was when I was sick in bed and home from school. I think I feigned a flu attack more than once to get the attention she normally was too busy to give.

My friends always loved her as she thrived on having people around, young and old. Though she was good to the people who worked for her, and the grocery clerks, the pharmacist, the person behind the counter at the dry cleaner's, when she decided that my newfound friend was "common," there was no changing her mind. She was, undeniably, a snob. We were taught never to use the word "drapes" for curtains or "folks" for one's family, "gown" for an evening dress or "tux" for a dinner coat. When she caught us chewing gum, she would stick out her hand, palm up under our chin and wait until we spit the wad into her hand. She insisted that Juicy Fruit gum (my favorite) smelled just like the air freshener in the ladies' room at the local gas station.

My Mother

After a few drinks, she and my father had loud arguments, but there is no doubt that they truly loved each other. She was the ideal co-dependent for my father and not once did I hear her scold him for having misbehaved the night before. She was diagnosed with cancer in 1966 and bravely fought it for seven years. One afternoon two weeks before she died, I sat at the end of her bed and we talked about life. We knew, she knew, that she didn't have much longer, so I told her of our many escapades, mostly Carolan's and mine. Though she seemed shocked by some of my stories, I don't think she was really surprised. It was one of the most powerful few hours of my life. I felt closer to her during that time than I ever had. It was a rare opportunity for closure that I'm thankful to have had. She died at age 56.

Daddy

My father was a good man—shy, loyal and honest, with a great sense of humor. My sister-in-law said it well when she described him as was one of those rare people who, when he entered a room, he thought, "There you are!" rather than "Here I am!" He truly cared about people. Unfortunately, he had a problem with alcohol. There have been many stories told about him over the years, as he had a way of becoming mischievous after drinking, doing the kinds of things other people find funny and hard to believe. The tales, highly embellished over the years, are now famous/infamous "Po stories," and great entertainment for many, but his capers were never malicious or at the expense of others. He had the instinctive ability to preserve his friendships, no matter what he did while under the influence.

My Father

I am still embarrassed when I hear the stories, though I'd probably think they were funny, too, if they weren't about my own father. Most of his stunts, of which we were thankfully oblivious at the time, were performed in the presence of his contemporaries. One incident involved a can of red paint. He came home late one night after a party, drove into the garage, and stepped out of the car into an open can of red paint. Being oblivious to anything, he never thought to take off his shoe. He tracked the paint from the garage, down the gravel driveway and into the house! The red shoe prints were still visible, though somewhat faded, the day we moved from 250 Roblar 20 years later.

One night he and my mother had a dinner party, with 8 or 10 of their good friends. After the usual lengthy cocktail hour, they sat down to dinner. His closest friend, a devilish sort, bet my father that he couldn't fit through the space where one of us, many years prior, had kicked out a small glass pane in the lower corner of the door that connected the hall and the dining room. The glass had been missing for years, but, as I mentioned, my mother had given up, never bothering to have it repaired. His squeezing through the narrow space appeared to be an impossible feat so they all placed their bets. He stood up, removed all of his clothes except his boxer shorts, and after much maneuvering, he came out the other side $250 richer. Still in his boxer shorts, and with our housekeeper Willie Mae barely blinking an eye, dinner was served. I still hear of his escapades and find it quite amazing he survived them.

When my mother died, my father was totally lost. He eventually recovered from his loss and married the widow of his good friend. Sue was chic, polished and good to us, his children . . . for a while. I suspect the shift in her attitude towards us was caused by jealousy, which, I've learned, is the root of most familial resentments. My father had a good relationship with all three of us, our spouses and our children and maybe gave us more attention than Sue thought acceptable. Another factor may have been that she was a gin drinker. She was living proof that the juniper berry has a toxic effect on most people and certainly on those around them.

She began chipping away at us one at a time, starting

16

with me. After the initial assault, I learned to keep my distance and in time Harry and Carolan followed suit after their own encounters with her. Her late husband's family owned an enormous old chateau in Switzerland and she had bought a beautiful house in the same town. She and my father spent a lot of time there and Carolan and I were invited to visit them in the fall of 1984. We were treated well. We all traveled together and had a good month with them, but we knew to tread lightly as we never knew when she was going to lash out at one of us. She died in 1989.

Not long after Sue's death, Daddy courted another strong-willed widow. Women loved him! In 1991 his amazingly resilient constitution finally gave out. During his final days we stood watch in his hospital room. His dearest friend, "Hookie," was there daily. Even up to the time when Daddy could barely speak, the two old friends continued to tease one another as only best friends do. It was very touching. Throughout his life he had a number of very close friends, some he'd known since elementary school, many from high school and college. My brother, sister and I were fortunate to have learned from him the importance and appreciation of close friendships. There is no question that my friends, many whom I've known for over 60 years, remain among my greatest treasures.

Carolan

Me & Carolan
First Communion, 1949

My sister, Carolan, and I were unusually close and we did everything together. We even shared many friends, rare for siblings with a two-year age difference. Sure, we fought as do all sisters, but we really loved one another. Though it was obvious that she was favored by my father, I never held it against her. Our sibling battles would always end with her—older, louder and bigger—the winner, and my retribution was to call her "Beautiful Carolan." For days after, if I needed or wanted anything from her, it had to be preceded by, "Please, Beautiful Carolan."

We dreamed up games of all sorts and there's no doubt that she made up the rules, which I never thought to question. It was all fun rather than competitive. One of our contests was for each of us to recite, in front of the other, the "Pledge of Allegiance" with a straight face—no smiling or laughing allowed. If, while reciting, we were guilty of anything other than deadpan, we had to start again from the beginning. I always went first and never got through the whole pledge without having to begin again, so it meant that she never even got tested.

Me & Carolan
Ovando, Montana, 2003

"Rain Hats"
Compliments of Sun Valley Lodge, 1996

Another contest involved our carrying the other, piggy-back, around a "course" which went from the bathroom, out into the hall, through the bedroom and back into the bathroom. Of course, I had to carry her first and she weighed considerably more than I did in those days. The rule was that if I touched or even barely brushed the wall with any part of her body while I carried her, I had to apologize to Beautiful Carolan and begin the rounds again. As in the first game, she never lost. We usually picked the nights my parents were having dinner guests to play the piggy-back game and "Soap the Bathroom," which required our pouring soap and water on the bathroom floor tiles and skating barefoot across the bathroom floor. It's a miracle we didn't kill ourselves, falling over one another and often landing in the bathtub or on the floor. As our bathroom

20

was directly above the dining room, I can still hear my enraged father apologizing to their guests, then yelling at the top of his lungs, "WHAT are you girls DOING up there?" We'd wait until he calmed down and soap the floor again!

Carolan now lives in Ketchum, Idaho, with two of her three children and three grandchildren living nearby.

Harry

Growing up, I barely knew my brother Harry. He worked in obscure places during the summers: a fish cannery in Alaska, an iron foundry in Half Moon Bay, and as a page in the Capitol in Sacramento. During the school year he was enough older than I to make me invisible to him and his friends. He lived in a room outside the main house, originally the "ice house," which lived up to its name. It was cold and damp, and I was rarely allowed to go near it, which was fine with me. He and my sister, only a year apart, would have horrendous fights at the dinner table. He had the ability to push her buttons, resulting in flying china and silverware and both of them being sent to their rooms. Often, Carolan and I would wait until my father came home from work, then provoke Harry, just to hear my father shout, "Harry! Will you stop needling the girls!" It was so satisfying to hear him get the blame as we innocently stood by. In later years, after attending prep school in Massachusetts, Harry returned to California to enter Stanford and it wasn't until his fraternity brothers started asking my sister and me to their parties that he finally acknowledged that he had two sisters.

Carolan, Harry & Me
Ovando, Montana, 2003

Harry and his wife, Cindy, have a wonderful ranch outside of Ovando, Montana on the North fork of the Blackfoot River. Their property has, aside from the main house, three cabins, which are constantly filled with friends and family from June through October. Cindy is a masterful cook, gardener and hostess and everyone wants to visit whenever possible—and we all do!

Harry & Cindy's Ranch
Ovando, Montana

Harry & Cindy's 20th Anniversary
Ovando, Montana, 2007

Tahoe

Our days at Tahoe were lazy and uncomplicated. Our house was one of eight on Sunnyside Lane, nestled among the pine trees. Ours was a rustic brown-shingled treasure with green trim, a summer house built in the early 1920s for my grandmother. It had its own distinct cool, piney fragrance with seven small bedrooms upstairs and a two-bedroom cottage, though the three rooms over the kitchen (maids' rooms) were no bigger than large closets. The other bedrooms weren't much bigger, with barely room for two narrow metal beds, a dresser and a chair. The two master/guest rooms at either end of the house were roomier. They all had views of the lake. It was a treasure.

Sunnyside Lane Tahoe House

Intro to Willie Mae/Tahoe

My parents had had a series of nanny/housekeepers but none could hold a candle to Willie Mae. She came to us when I was eight and basically saved my life in more ways than one. Upon her arrival she was immediately endeared to me as she was the only one in the family who didn't call me "piglet." Her first experience with us was a trip to Lake Tahoe. We jammed her (all 260 pounds) into the back seat of my mother's Chevrolet, along with two dogs, two cats, my sister and me and all the stuffed animals, ceramic figures and junk we felt we couldn't live without during our six weeks at Tahoe. My mother drove, how I'll never know, but it was part of the yearly routine and she didn't complain. My father would fly up on Fridays, land on the lake in a commercial seaplane, and take off again on Monday morning, leaving Mom to deal with the weekday crises. We became well acquainted with Willie Mae during that first six-hour drive to Tahoe. Once we got there, it didn't take long for her to decide that she hated Tahoe. She was terrified of "the bears" (no one had seen one in years), wouldn't go outside after dusk and wouldn't set foot anywhere near the water. It's surprising that, after such a miserable "trial period," she agreed to take the job as our new housekeeper at 250 Roblar, but only on the condition that she would not be required to go to Tahoe again.

After that summer, my mother made sure we had a substitute housekeeper to accompany us to Tahoe. She hired the wife of one of the farm workers at my grandmother's ranch who adjusted well to life at Tahoe. In fact, maybe too well. One day she asked me to take her out in the canoe. In my normal careless way, I never even thought about life jackets. We weren't on the water more than five minutes before we tipped over. That's when I learned that she did not know how to swim! I tried to save her but she dragged me under. The next thing I knew, I was standing on the dock yelling for help. How I got there, I'll never know; but a neighbor heard my screams, ran over and pulled her out of the water.

While reminiscing about life at Tahoe, I flash back to one of my father's most notable rituals. Every morning he would arise while we were still tucked in, and with his dogs, he would go down to the pier, dive into the 50+ degree water, and stay in just long enough to become numb. He would then return to the bathroom we shared, remove his frozen swimming trunks, open the window over the tub that looked out over the lake, and throw them out the window, aiming for the warm flagstone patio two stories below. Plop! He then would sink into the steaming hot tub, reading his book for what seemed like hours as we waited in line for the bathroom. By the time he emerged from the cooled bath water, the swimming trunks on the patio below were dry, "pressed" by the sun and maybe a little faded. My father—the unknowing creator of the "shabby chic" look.

In those days Tahoe City consisted of no more than one narrow two-lane road with no stoplights, a post office, a bakery, and the Village Store, a family-owned grocery and meat market/clothing/variety/drug store, the only one in town. It was the meeting place for locals and summer residents alike. Tahoe was simple, pristine and uncrowded. The only place on the lake that had a hint of tackiness was King's Beach, which remains today exactly as it did then. Tahoe had no mail delivery service so part of one's daily routine was to pick up the mail at the General Delivery window at the Tahoe City post office.

When making a phone call from our house, one would pick up the receiver and wait to hear a friendly voice, "Operator. May I help you?" Our number was "Tahoe City 48." There were party lines in those days and I am sure the friendly voice got an earful. We would swim from pier to pier in the icy water, catching "crawlfish" and winding our way, always barefoot, through the woods and over the two-lane highway to the little store that sat in front of Mayhew's Ward Creek Cottages. Mrs. Mayhew and her daughter, Barbara, registered their overnight guests at the store counter where we hung out, pestering them with countless questions, reading the comic books but never buying them.

The store carried all the essentials: ice cream, candy, gum, crème soda, comic books and movie magazines. At the beginning of every summer, we were each given a $5 allowance to spend however we wished. We chose to take out separate charge accounts at Mayhew's and "run up a tab" like the grown-ups. We never spent a cent on comic books, it all went to candy and gum. With the help of generous hand-outs from the Mayhews, our allowance lasted the entire six weeks.

Secret Harbor

The Viking . . . Timeless!

On weekends my father would crank up the engine on his beloved "Viking," a historic 42-foot antique boat that in earlier times had served as the mail boat between San Pedro and Catalina Island. We would chug across the lake to Secret Harbor, a magical place founded back in the 1920s by six families, including ours. The original price for six lakefront acres was $3,563. In 1951, 40 additional acres were purchased for $4,500. The original families still own it and the majority of its members treasure it and do what they can to protect it.

Secret Harbor remains the only "untouched" property at Tahoe today. (Everything around it has been developed). It stands today exactly as it did back in the

1920s with a few added amenities. It has a pristine sandy beach with picnic tables that, depending upon the volume of water in the lake each year, sit near or at water's edge. Above the beach are scattered over 40 acres, six separate camps, each one with running water and a built-in barbeque, and flushing toilets within walking distance from each camp. Though it isn't exactly roughing it, this is where we learned, at an early age, to appreciate camping. The cove is surrounded by huge granite rocks perfect for high-diving.

Secret Harbor

Most often we would go over just for the day and spend all day diving off the rocks, swimming to the buoy, and tipping over the canoe. Due to the shallow sandy bottom inside the harbor, the water is 10+ degrees warmer than that on the other side of the lake. Our mother would prepare "purple onion" sandwiches, barbequed hamburgers, or both, for us while she, my father and their friends had multiple gin-and-tonics. The "G and T's" seemed like fun for awhile, but didn't do much for my father's mood by the time we were ready to head home. Our trips back across the lake were precarious—we learned to retreat to the bow of the boat and stay out of his way. Battling the afternoon westerly swells was a challenge for even the most seasoned of sailors, so it was always a miracle that we made it home.

"Harry's Happy Camp"
Secret Harbor, 1988

Once we returned to Hillsborough at the end of Willie Mae's first summer with us, it became clear that she would become part of our family. Though she had a husband, Bennie, who lived in San Francisco (and weighed less than half her weight), she lived with us, along with her dog, Tuffy, and would go home to Bennie on Thursdays and Sundays. Our friends loved her and would make a point of stopping by our house on the way to school while we chased, teased and laughed with her. She never allowed us to go off to school without a big warm hug for each of us. We nicknamed her "Weasel" and she loved it. We would have contests to see who could last the longest with all 260 pounds of Willie Mae sitting on them in the rocking chair in the kitchen. On her days off she would eat pork and turnip greens, which were certain to make her sick, but she just couldn't give them up. She often complained of "cadillacs" in her eyes and suffered from "the misery," but she just kept going. She was a great cook and made sure we were all well-fed. She taught us how to play poker and when my parents went out (almost every night), Willie Mae would engage us in a mean poker game.

But it wasn't always fun and games—one cold and rainy afternoon when I was in elementary school I came in soaking wet after playing with friends. Hoping to get warm, I stood by the stove, warming my hands over the burner. Before I knew it, my shirt caught fire. I felt the heat and reached back to feel the flames. My instinctive reaction was to try to run from the fire so I took off through the dining room and headed for the front door. Luckily, Willie Mae had been in the kitchen, ironing, and had caught a glimpse of what had happened. She ran after me and literally tackled me, rolling me on the dining room carpet, putting out the flames. If it hadn't been for her, I would have suffered more than singed hair and second and third degree burns on my hands, arm and back.

After my sister and brother were sent off to boarding school, my parents travelled a lot and Willie Mae was my anchor. I'm not sure where I would be today if it hadn't been for her. And when we got older, we had friends who would come up from Stanford and, after a rum toddy or two, off they'd go to the horse races with Willie Mae at the wheel. She was indeed a classic! I look back on those years and wish that I had done more for her after she left my parents and was unable to work any longer.

Johnny

Johnny & Me
On Our 60th Birthday, 2002

It happens that Johnny and I were born on the same day in 1942—Johnny in New York and I in Pasadena. We were thrown together in 1949 when his parents, close friends of my parents, moved to California from New Jersey. We had a special bond from the very beginning. We became fast friends and were inseparable for more than three years before his parents divorced and his mother moved him and his siblings back to New York.

I was heartbroken when Johnny left, but he spent summers and some Christmas vacations in California with his father, so we never lost touch. It was uncanny how we could pick up right where we'd left off at the end of his previous visit. He returned to San Francisco in the 1960s and we've remained close friends all these years. Though we have chosen different lifestyles, we have a rare understanding, a certain kinship that often occurs between people who share a birthday.

We've celebrated many birthdays together. Now that he lives in Puerto Vallarta for most of the year, I visit him there, and love being there to observe his obvious contentment. He's found his niche. Whenever we get together, we reminisce about our childhood adventures— not only were we resourceful, but how did we get away with so much? One of our more creative ways to make a few dollars, after becoming bored with the humdrum lemonade stand, was to sneak into our neighbors' yards, pick flowers from their gardens, arrange them into neat little bouquets and sell them door-to-door to the very neighbors who had grown them! Somehow we were able to arrange the flowers so their owners had no idea they'd just been picked from their own precious gardens. They thought we were so cute!

Another source of instant cash which required door-to-door sales was a stash of tiny square-ish old bottles of strong-smelling bath(?) oil we'd found in Johnny's father's attic. They must have been discarded years before by his grandmother or previous homeowner. Johnny, the consummate salesperson, had quite a story to tell about these rare bottles of French perfume and we made enough money to keep us well-supplied with candy, comic books and other goods our parents frowned upon.

Our trips to downtown San Mateo didn't change much from day to day, the only difference being the players we'd choose to join us each day. On our way to 3rd Avenue, we would stop off at 10 DeSabla Road, the 11-story apartment building, a skyscraper to us in those days, where my grandmother lived. We would take the elevator to the basement where there was a laundry room with washers and dryers for the tenants. We would find some poor soul's unaccompanied laundry, either in the dryer or sitting in a basket, take it by elevator to the top floor where there was a lovely roof garden, and throw each item off the balcony, one piece at a time, and watch it float lazily down to the street. When the basket was empty, we'd head down the elevator and go directly across the street to Mills Hospital, where, in the basement was a huge vat of boiling hot paraffin. (We never did learn what it was used for.) We'd each dip one arm into it, up to the elbow, lift it out long enough to let it set, dip it back in two or three times, and *voila*!—we had our own arm cast—a way, we thought, to get sympathy from the downtown merchants upon whom we were about to descend. Our first stop was the City of Paris, where there was Mitzi who wore white gloves and operated the elevator. She went along with our arm cast charade, never letting on that she knew just what we'd been up to. We would ride up and down that elevator for hours. It seemed that she was amused by us but I think that we were just a diversion for her as her job had to be tedious, up and down day in and day out.

Johnny and I were the proud founders of "The Jolly Club," which consisted of 8-10 members, all of them our classmates. I don't remember exactly what the criteria for acceptance was, but most of the potential members lived in nice houses and I suspect their admission had something to do with the quality of the club room they had to offer when it was their turn to host the meeting. 250 Roblar never would have passed the test, but being the founders, Johnny and I were excused from having to provide the club room, refreshments, or even dues. I don't think that Suzi's house would have passed under our guidelines either, but her older brother had a neat clubhouse in the basement and was willing to loan it to us for our meetings. For a fee, of course.

Me & Suzi

& Andra

After Johnny left, I spent my time with two friends in particular, Suzi and Andra. Suzi was cute, petite, very smart and blonde. Andra was a pretty, tall, slender brunette. There I was, in the middle, medium-round, holding my own by being the instigator of practical pranks.

Andra & Suzi, 1954

Kindergarten
Hillsborough School, 1947

One afternoon after school, Andra and I headed to downtown San Mateo for the usual: a stop by the drugstore to read, not buy, the latest comic books, head next door to the local jeweler, with whom we flirted and pestered until he politely asked us to leave, then go into Benny's Market, where my mother had a charge account. Each of us would fill up a bag with candy, lollipops, bubblegum and corn-nuts and walk up and down the streets saying hello and waving to anyone coming our way. The more attractive the person, the friendlier we were. One man, very tall, handsome and unusually well-dressed for San Mateo, smiled and waved back, seemingly amused, as he passed by. Later that afternoon, we returned to my house, opened the front door, and there in the living room stood that very same well-dressed man! He looked at us, we looked at him, and he very nicely said, "Aren't you the young ladies who waved at me in San Mateo this afternoon?" My parents were even more stunned than we were. He was the Headmaster of the fancy prep school in Massachusetts that my father had attended and my brother was hoping to attend!

Andra and I were such close friends her parents agreed to let her join me at boarding school, the Dominican Convent in San Rafael. She decided after our sophomore year that she could no longer take life in captivity and returned to the local public high school where she was much happier.

New Friends

About that time, I met a new group of kids my age, all living in Hillsborough and attending private schools. They accepted me with open arms. I had never before received the kind of male attention as I did at that time and I was swept away by it. Though I'm not proud of it, with all of this newfound attention, I had little time for my longtime childhood friends. My new friends lived in the fashionable part of Hillsborough, every one in a big house with a full staff. There were countesses and one vicomtesse and everyone was related. Everyone, that is, but me. I was the only one who wasn't a deYoung, a deTristan, a deDampierre, a deSugny, a deGuigne or a deBonchamps!

I learned quickly that things are not always as glamorous as they might appear. Axel, whose mother was a countess, kept a pistol under his pillow and knives in his dresser drawer. I would never have known what a Luger pistol is if it hadn't been for him. He was an interesting, amusing, though eccentric character, and he took a liking to me, showing his affection by hitting me in the stomach with his tennis racquet or pushing me, fully clothed, into the swimming pool. Axel's mother, the countess, had a pet skunk named "Fancy." She also had a large tortoise, not housebroken, who roamed the downstairs of their chateau. When we visited them we never knew who we'd step on or what we'd step in but it was never boring.

Axel, 1959

One summer afternoon Axel and his cousin thought it would be fun to put me and a friend (another cousin) into the trunk of his car and take us up to the private estate owned by yet another cousin and let us out there. Of course, we thought it was great fun but allowed them to believe that we were terrified. They dropped us off, and when they came back to get us, we hid from them. They searched for us until after dark and, in a state of panic, even recruited a number of our friends to assist in the search. We let them stew until later that night when we finally admitted that earlier in the afternoon we'd made our way home and had been safe and sound for hours. The joke was on them.

Peter

My first real love, Peter, was one of the leaders of the group. I didn't think he'd even noticed me but soon we were known as the ideal couple and we spent four years together. He was kind, well-mannered and fun loving. He was very good to me and I often wondered if I deserved him. He lived in a lovely house and I spent most of my time there. There were sit-down dinners with his parents, where he was required to wear coat and tie, and I was very thankful for the training I'd received at my grandmother's Sunday night dinners. We were served by a little Japanese couple and I was afraid to open my mouth at the table though his parents were gracious and kind to me. The only time I can remember Peter being anything but gentle with me was when I was commissioned to cut his hair, a regular free service I rendered to all of my male friends. This time the cheap kitchen shears failed me and Peter's head was left with numerous bare spots. He was forced to rely on the local barber to repair the damage which left him nearly bald.

Me & Peter
Beta Theta Pi Christmas Formal
Berkeley, 1960

Our entire group spent some wonderful, carefree summers either at "the club," (Burlingame Country Club), at Tahoe, lounging around their families' swimming pools, or driving around in their cars. This often led to mischief. One summer we planned a party at the house of one of the boys whose parents were out of town. We invited friends from Marin and San Francisco, as well as the local regulars.

Peter had been given a Model T truck by his godfather, so we filled up the back of it with cans of beer and ice, backed it up to the front door of the "party house" and proceeded to have quite a time for ourselves, eating, drinking, singing and dancing. We finished off the beer and the contents of the absentee parents' liquor cabinet and decided to call it a night after one of the boys stuck his elbow through the plaster wall in the front hall.

The following day Peter and I returned to the scene to help clean up the mess. While taking a break from the patching, mopping, hosing, sweeping, I was leaning, or swinging, on the metal bar that held up the awning outside the living room. The telephone rang. Our party host, Mike, answered the call in the living room and at that very moment the awning, the connecting poles, everything, came crashing down through the plate glass window which stretched the entire length of the living room! Yes, it was his parents on the other end of the line! He had a pretty difficult time explaining what had just happened. Fortunately, no one was injured, his parents never found out about the party, the insurance company took care of the window and I never heard another word about it.

July was the month we all spent together at Tahoe. Many of my friends' parents rented big old historic houses for the summer with boats included, though most of the boys had boats of their own. We spent every day water skiing and tossing each other off the piers and into the water. The boys became so adept at water skiing, they often skied six at a time, behind one boat with each one on a single ski. The tourists loved it. I was never totally comfortable in a bathing suit or on water skis. I was perfectly happy wearing my Bermuda shorts, riding in the boat and manning the ski ropes, but Peter insisted that I didn't look fat in a bathing suit and, with much patience he taught me to master one ski.

That particular July one well-bred family from San Francisco rented the house two doors down from ours. Every day we were invited to have lunch there, a sit-down gourmet affair, served by Adrian the butler. The only requirement was that we wear shirts over our bathing suits. The parents were often in attendance. After they excused themselves we would stay around to have contests to see who could fit the largest number of grapes into our mouths. This resulted in some pretty unattractive drooling and gagging, so we found more refined ways to amuse ourselves. At night we would attend movies at the old Tahoe Tavern. Directly below the movie theater was the bowling alley, so, throughout the movie you could hear the bowling balls hitting the pins as if we were all in the same room. In those days, we weren't paying much attention to the movie anyway. Not long after that the Tavern was condemned as a "firetrap" and razed to make room for condominiums. I still have vivid memories of that wonderful old place, with its porches lined with paper Chinese lanterns. It was like stepping back into the 1920s.

Me, Peter, Lynn Bradley, Rusty Hale
Kellogg Mines, Idaho, 1959

Dead-End Kids

One afternoon when we were all home from school for the holidays, we thought it would be fun to stage a fake murder in front of the movie theater on Burlingame Avenue. After much scheming and planning, two of us, acting as an innocent couple, approached the ticket booth as if we were about to buy tickets for the afternoon show.

Just as my date was about to pay, a beat-up Oldsmobile drove by very slowly and the driver "shot" him (with a fake cap gun) in front of the ticket booth. He crumbled to the ground and I ran. Two guys dressed in corset-tight, above-the-knee, size "small" trench coats (borrowed from my sister's and my closets), jumped out of the back seat, dragged the injured/dead man to the car, stuffed him into the trunk (with one arm purposely hanging out) and drove off.

I guess we were better actors than we thought. We had caused a major panic among the bystanders and the merchants. In the meantime, the bad guys drove around the corner and picked me up. We thought we had pulled it off, undetected. To us, it was just a lark, but the Burlingame police were not amused. We had our hands slapped and we promised never to pull that stunt again. To this day, I believe the juvenile mobsters were saved from harsh punishment by having been born into the right Hillsborough families. From then on we were known as "the dead-end kids."

Peter's Model-T was finally confiscated by the Hillsborough Police Department after we took it for a spin through the middle of the carefully planted and city-maintained islands separating the roads in San Mateo Park, knocking down a stop sign or two in our path. Finally, we realized that wanton destruction wasn't funny to anyone but us so we dreamed up a slightly more innocent scheme. One summer day, I was the only female, as was often the case, so I was the appointed driver. Five not-so-small guys,

Letter from Commander Ernie Lena,
Hillsborough Police Department,
Regarding the Offenses Committed 20 Years Earlier
by the Dead End Kids

dressed in swimming trunks, piled into the back of a station wagon, mapped out their route to random houses with swimming pools, and I was given directions and told when to stop the car. I followed orders, stopped when I was told, they climbed out the back of the car, scaled the fence surrounding the pool, dove into the pool, swam the length, got out, climbed back over the fence and into the back of the car, and off we'd go to the next address. Unfortunately, I was never able to see the stunned expressions on the faces of the people relaxing around their pools, but I guess the looks were worthy of photographs! We would cover four or five pools a day, three years running, and never were apprehended. It seems most of the pools' owners were good natured, and at one final stop the boys heard one man, obviously amused, saying as he saw them coming over the fence, "Oh no! Here they come again!"

Dominican

Life was not all carefree summers and vacation experiences. My four years at the Dominican Convent can only be described as a learning experience. As my sister had preceded me by two years, I thought I knew what to expect, but I really had no idea. The rules were many, archaic and very strict. For us mischievous types, these rules were made only to be broken. Leaving campus without a chaperone, chewing gum, smoking or, God forbid, drinking, could result in permanent dismissal, depending upon the violator's general attitude.

"Attitude" was the key word in all aspects of Dominican life. We succeeded in breaking all of the rules and lived to tell about it upon graduating. The Dominicans were known as a teaching order. Though they lived up to it, our nuns seemed to be more intent upon turning us into respectable young ladies than intellectuals. We had endless courtesy classes with our guideline, the little black "Courtesy Book," written back in the dark ages by one of the nuns. While in the refectory for meals, there was always a nun standing watch to remind us to sit up straight, not to reach across the table or to talk with our mouth full. There was even a "fat table," to which I was assigned the first month I was at Dominican and Carolan, the last month of her four years there.

On occasion someone would be asked to leave the dining room for having committed some unconscionable offense like making faces or waving to someone at another table. We were on our best behavior during lunch as that's when we received our anxiously awaited mail. Our outgoing mail was censored but I had a different plan for my letters to Peter. I would ask to borrow a day student's English book, slip the letter between the pages and return the book to her. She would gladly mail the letter on her way home from school. On Sunday nights we were required to attend concerts, with the intention of instilling in us some music appreciation. Painfully bored, we would write letters on the backs of the concert programs as we sat in the darkened hall. Those letters went out with the day students as well.

Receiving a package was one of the highlights of life at Dominican. Parents would send care packages; cookies, candy, new socks, but nobody's care package could compare to those I got from Johnny. He attended Brooks School, a prestigious prep school on the East Coast, and was not happy there, so he amused himself by sending me full sets of Brooks' finest china, stolen from the school dining room, a mangy old bear rug head sporting one glass eye and a pink porcelain tongue that fell out, a real, flattened pancake and other treasures. The nuns had to have been entertained by Johnny's resourcefulness, but God forbid they show it!

Every Saturday we had an assembly where we received "conduct cards," delivered individually to each student by our principal, Sister Maurice. We were reprimanded for being less than perfect in front of the entire student body. Our every move was regulated by a system of demerits, recorded on these little white cards. There were five listed categories, among them Neatness, Courtesy, Punctuality and Attitude. What you wanted to avoid were demerits in Attitude. The perfect person, with no demerits, got an 'A' card. An A- was given for having left a hair in one's hairbrush or a crease in her bedspread. A 'B' card was slightly more serious. I received my first B card the week after our first free weekend of my Freshman year. The Friday of our release, I was so excited to go home I left my room in total disarray, not thinking or caring about the consequences. The room inspector, Sister Carol, gave me a B card in "neatness." This was the first of my many lessons in learning that there is a price to pay for reckless abandon. Eventually it did sink in. Cleanliness fell under the neatness category. We were required to bathe every day and to check in with a sister and her little black book immediately after our bath. Failing to check in earned at least a minus in neatness. My junior-year roommate rarely saw an A- though she should have seen many as she would often skip her daily shower, wearing her bathrobe over her uniform and checking in with the rest of us who had adhered to the rules of hygiene. I never squealed on her but wished that someone would as our room had an unpleasant odor that could have easily been avoided with a little soap and water.

A 'C' card was not given out often and was frowned upon by even those of us less-than-perfect people because it meant the recipient was stupid/careless enough to get caught. Anything worse than a C card, you were out! Over the years, a few girls, mysteriously disappeared after a weekend at home or holiday break and we were not told what had happened to them. We learned later that there had been a few cases of serious anorexia and even a couple of unmentionable pregnancies. This of course was shocking to us as the word "sex" was never uttered let alone practiced by Dominican girls! Anorexia and bulimia were far more prevalent than any of us realized. We were obsessed with our weight and our main topic of conversation was dieting and food. It was as if we were setting the tone for the Twiggy era.

Sister Maurice ruled with an iron fist and controlled us by having us believe that she was a wicked, unreasonable woman. She put the fear of God into us the day we entered the hallowed halls as freshmen and did her best to keep it there by growling, "Wipe that smile off your face!" or "Go upstairs and polish those shoes!" But many of us learned by the middle of our senior year that there was a warm heart under that habit and she would invite us into her once-forbidding office for late night chats. I was not a great student. I had a difficult time concentrating and was much more interested in what was going on around me than in the book before me. I am fairly certain I had ADD, a disorder that was unheard of in those days, let alone treated. At one point I was struggling with Algebra, so Sister Maurice, being the Algebra I teacher, asked one of her prize pupils and a close friend of mine, to tutor me, privately and secretly. I'm not sure it did much good but it helped a lot to know they both wanted to see me succeed.

We were allocated one free weekend a month to either go home or to go home with a classmate, pending of course, approval from Sister Maurice. On Sundays we were allowed to go out from 11-4 provided we had adult supervision. A couple of day students' mothers were sympathetic and would pick us up, then leave us to our own devices, which for me often meant meeting up with Peter and our friends. I think that Sister Maurice was onto this, but she thought so highly of Peter (after all, he had been elected President of the student body at Bellarmine, the reputable Jesuit-run college prep, so he must be OK), she went along with the charade. Sheila lived just around the corner from school and her mother was our most loyal ally. Not only would she rescue us on Sundays, but I would spend weeks during the summers at the Gradys' and, though she was wise to our many misdeeds, she would pretend she didn't know what we were up to. I spent a lot of time in Marin and there I discovered a whole new set of dead-end kids.

Peter Rabbit

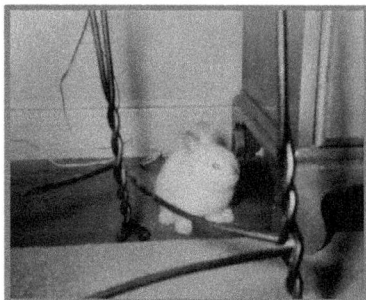

The Infamous Peter Rabbit, 1959

I did a lot of much-needed growing up at boarding school and finally by the fourth year the nuns rarely found cause to scold me—maybe because by that time I had learned the ropes and there were plenty of unruly freshmen, like I had been, who needed the attention. By then they considered most of our pranks (those that they were aware of) minor and they pretty much overlooked them. One that they could not ignore was the 'Adventure of Peter Rabbit.' During Christmas vacation of my senior year, Peter and I had been driving home from a friend's parents' Cloverdale ranch when we spotted a sign, "Bunnies for Sale." We stopped just to take a look. They were only a few weeks old and irresistible. Peter picked out the cutest one and he bought it for me.

When it was time to return to school, the bunny went with me. Well, a pet of any kind wasn't even an option at Dominican so we had to keep him hidden. In fact, no one was ever known to have even considered bringing a pet to school. My roommate, Julie, had a cedar chest and Peter

Rabbit lived inside it when we were not in our room. How he was not discovered during our twice-daily room inspections, I'll never know. When we were present he ran free. Our few classmates who'd been let in on our secret were amazed we were able to pull it off. They spent every free minute in our room cuddling this adorable forbidden creature.

He/we prevailed until one night when Sister Aquinas unexpectedly visited our room. We didn't have time to hide him. She could not believe what she was seeing and I was ordered to get rid of him. Sister Aquinas never did have much of a sense of humor! Peter had a new home with my sister at 250 Roblar and surprisingly, I was not expelled. In fact, I didn't even receive a B card, probably because there was no category in the demerit book under which to charge me.

Julie

I made many lifelong friends at Dominican and though we complained about our imprisonment, the food, the rules, the nuns, I learned a lot and am thankful to have had those years there. In my senior year I was fortunate enough to have Julie as my roommate. She became one of my dearest friends and one of the best people I've ever known. Julie arrived as a freshman from a ranch in Walnut Grove. She was smart, soft-spoken and wiser than most of us. It didn't take long for us to look to her as a leader and for her to join us on some of our capers. She was a great co-conspirator as the nuns never suspected this innocent auburn-haired farm girl of doing anything untoward. After Dominican, she attended Stanford and we stayed in close touch during those years, often ending up at the same fraternity parties.

Julie & Me
California State Fair, 1957

After Graduation / Hawaii

We often look back on the summer after we graduated from Dominican. Sheila, Julie and I flew to Honolulu—graduation presents from our parents. We stayed with our two Hawaii-born classmates who lived next door to one another in Kahala, a lovely upscale neighborhood just outside of Honolulu. We spent every day at the beach and partied every night. We saw a side of Julie we'd not seen before and she had more fun than all of us put together. The father of one of our native classmates was the liquor distributor for the islands so we had a full bar at our disposal of which we took full advantage. Every 17-18-year-old in the area descended upon their house each evening and we partied into the wee hours, slept in the next morning, went to the beach and repeated the routine every evening.

We had originally been invited to stay for two weeks. I stayed for three and the other two stayed all summer. When my three weeks were up, I hated leaving but knew I had to go home. Peter met me at the airplane in San Francisco and I will never forget the look on his face as I stepped off the plane. I was 10 pounds heavier than when I'd left, had cut my hair into a way too-short pixie cut, and was wearing a muumuu and no shoes. Though he was not enamored by this what-me-worry stranger, he tolerated me and I eventually came around. My mother nearly disowned me.

(L-R) Myself, Barbara, Dina, Julie, Denby, Sheila, Boy?

(L-R) Barbara, Julie, Sheila, Me, Dina

Debutante

That same summer I received an invitation to be a San Francisco Debutante, a given for descendant daughters of California pioneers. When I saw the invitation, I immediately told my mother I didn't want to participate, though I knew this meant more to her than anything. My refusal went in one ear and out the other and I realized that the choice wasn't really mine to make. Though I was never totally comfortable with the concept, I don't deny that once I agreed to do it I had the time of my life. I was reluctant to ask Peter to be my escort as he was as rebellious as I was and I was sure he would not want to do it. I even offered to give him an out by suggesting I'd ask someone else but, surprisingly, he accepted my invitation without hesitation.

Every day the mailbox at 250 Roblar was stuffed with invitations to luncheons, teas, barbeques and all-night balls. For the first time in my life my mother agreed to buy me some new dresses and appropriate "deb attire," as opposed to the usual hand-me-downs. We were busy with events most days and every night. During September, before we all left for college, there was a grand ball every night. These were often given either in the ballroom of the home of the honoree, at a palatial estate belonging to her grandparents or at the Burlingame Country Club. The party never started before 10:00 PM and went full-blown until dawn. There were tables that stretched as far as you could see, covered with platters of every delectable dish one could imagine, a full bar in every corner and music by world-renowned orchestras, who were relieved during their breaks by the latest "pop" band.

All of these events were topped in December by the Cotillion, the Ball at which the debs are "presented to society." For this we were required to wear full-length white ball gowns and long white gloves. I was fortunate to have been offered the loan of a dress, handmade for and worn two years earlier by the daughter of one of my mother's friends. It was made of hundreds of hand-sewn pleats of chiffon running horizontally from top to bottom. It was beautiful. But after the usual first-year-of-college weight gain, every seam had to be let out and on the big night it was so tight I could barely breathe.

The evening itself was a spectacle. As each of us was presented, our full name was announced, we walked out onto a spotlighted platform, and there we would perform the much rehearsed curtsy. We then continued down what seemed to be a thousand steps. At the bottom of the steps our escorts were waiting and the parade began, winding through the Grand Ballroom and two or three other massive rooms of the Palace Hotel. As I have never been one to enjoy the spotlight, that part was not a pleasant experience for me, but the evening passed quickly. After feigning the obligatory waltz with our escorts, or fathers and a few other white tie, tailed relatives, four of us were happy to sneak out early to drive to Sugar Bowl for New Year's.

Marin/Mik

I also spent a lot of time that summer with the Marin dead-enders, where we invented and attended numerous beer-infused "hill parties," smoked cigarettes, drove around in Sheila's convertible and worked on our tans. Mik played a leading role here, and I mention him specifically because he was a true character and because he was the inspiration for me to write my story.

In December of 2008, Mik very suddenly passed away in his sleep. While we were all in shock and totally disheartened, his wife Suzi asked me if I would speak at the "Celebration of Mik's Life" to be held a few weeks later. I wasn't sure that I would be able to hold back my emotions in front of all those people, but of course I accepted. I've always been terrified of public speaking but I was deeply honored to have been asked, and while speaking about Mik I was able to put the fear aside and got totally into the details of a few of our escapades.

I sat down to compose a few words for Mik and I realized then that I had SO many stories to tell that needed to be told. After relating Mik's story and reflecting upon my charmed, privileged and never-dull life, I began writing this book.

One of the stories I told took place in the early 1960s in the East Bay where one of our Marin friends had taken a summer job. We'd all gathered for dinner at his apartment. There was plenty of Coors on hand and when dinner was "on the table," our steaks were literally on the table—there were no plates. After dinner we moved outside for an impromptu "street party," when a neighbor spotted Mik in his seersucker Bermuda shorts and reported to the police that he was running down the street in his underwear.

The police showed up. We all scattered and Mik and I ended up huddled together behind a tree. When spotlighted by the police Mik told me to "act like a statue, like this," as he stood on one foot, took the ballet position with his arms in the air, facing skyward and forming his lips into a spout position. He was certain he looked like the perfect fountain, but not so . . . off we went in the back seat of the police car. After 15 minutes of Mik's notorious gibberish, the officer let us go, saying he'd been called to assist in a nearby accident, but I think he had never had anyone like Mik sitting behind him, was disarmed and so totally amused by him, he didn't have the heart to arrest us. Another close call. I told a few more funny stories about Mik that day but, more than that, I was proud to have had the opportunity to acknowledge the many good deeds he performed behind the scenes every day, the little things he did for others, never seeking recognition. Mik was one in a million and is sorely missed by everyone who knew him.

Colorado/Stanford

After graduating from Dominican I attended the University of Colorado, went through sorority rush and pledged Kappa Alpha Theta. Somehow I was elected President of my second semester pledge class—not as impressive as it sounds, as we were the flunkies, the pledges from first semester who had not made our grades. I knew from the moment I arrived in Boulder that it had been a mistake for me to jump from my strict convent years into this unstructured life of total freedom. I did attend most of my classes, unless . . . an invitation to go skiing came my way. It did take preference over Western Civilization.

Me & Dick Weisman
Kappa Alpha Theta Pledge Formal
Denver, Colorado, 1959

My academic performance was far from stellar and I stayed only one year. I returned to Ma Poett's and spent that summer with a part-time job in a dress shop and the rest of my time with the dead-end kids. Carolan was also living at home then and our adventures were many. That fall I attended secretarial/business school and she worked in retail. We spent a lot of time at Stanford attending football games and fraternity parties, often double-dating.

One evening we had agreed to go out with two brothers, both Stanford students. Not long before they were scheduled to pick us up we received a call from some other Stanford students, asking us to join them at a party in Marin County. We found the second invitation far more appealing so we accepted, and left a note on the front door telling the brothers that "something had come up" (the audacity!)

Five of us headed toward the party in Marin County and decided to take a detour into Sausalito for a quick drink. We were all under age, but fake IDs in those days were easily accessible and seldom questioned. Those few hours we spent in Sausalito were indelible. We started out at the "No Name Bar," (which remains in the same location today, with the same smoke-infused carpet, walls, and regular patrons 50 years later). At that time the police station was immediately next door, now the Sausalito branch of the Wells Fargo Bank.

We were enjoying our gin-and-tonics, until one of the spies from next door spotted us. My date and I, whom I'd not met before that evening, bolted, drinks in hand, when we saw the officer approaching. Immediately outside the front door of the bar sat an unattended long black limousine . . . with the keys in it. It was too tempting! The next thing I knew, my date was chauffeuring me, as I sat in the back seat sipping my G & T. We took a quick spin around the block and decided not to push our luck any further, abandoning the limo on Princess Street, not far from where we'd found it, and returned to the No Name. By that time our cohorts had been interrogated, "booked" and sent on their way. We gladly left Sausalito and headed toward home.

Then . . . remembering our original destination, the party, we attempted to make a U-turn on the Golden Gate bridge. We were stopped and pulled over by the Bridge Patrol. As the officer questioned our driver, we overheard on his radio, "the limousine has been found!" Little did he know that he was looking at the perpetrators! He scolded us for the U-turn, let us go and this time we headed south, giving up on the Marin party.

A few weeks later three scary men wearing badges showed up at 250 Roblar. It was the ABC (Alcoholic Beverage Control) asking for Carolan Poett. I knew right away who they were and why they were there and I made myself invisible. For at least an hour, with my parents as witnesses, they interrogated, and she, under oath, did her best to resurrect every detail of their evening at the No Name Bar. Luckily for me, they never associated the missing limousine with her group of underage delinquents and she never let on that my chauffeur and I had been part of her party. The scary men went away with her written confession in hand, and that was it. I'm not sure she ever forgave me for my not having been a part of the investigation, as my offense was certainly more serious than the one for which she'd been cited, but I believe she knows I would've done the same for her.

More Tahoe

That same summer Carolan and I took numerous trips to Tahoe in our pea-green 1952 Chrysler, a hand-me-down from Gammy. It had dark green velvet seats and a mint-green plastic steering wheel with white wiggly lines/veins, trying to look like marble I think. It drove like a truck but it served us well and we named it "Rodney." I was usually the designated driver, which was a wise choice, as Carolan was known to be far more interested in looking at her passenger(s) while driving than she was in watching the road.

One trip took us to Secret Harbor where, after a spring of fraternity parties, picnics, etc., we'd vowed to live a "clean life" for a week and possibly lose a few lbs. We loaded up with fruits, vegetables, protein, very little clothing and a pile of books and magazines and headed for our retreat site. Within two days we were so bored with the program, we caved in by going into King's Beach, buying enough junk food to last us the rest of the week and stopping by a small Tahitian-style bar for a rum drink or two for the ride back into Secret. So much for the Poett 7-day-weight-loss-program. Though we failed there, we met our other goals: a week of swimming, sunning, reading, no telephones, no one to answer to and few, sometimes no clothes! We had the entire place to ourselves, tucked away in one of the most beautiful places in the world, with not a care. How fortunate we were.

Andre

**Me, Grand-mere, Andre, Willie Mae
Carolan's Wedding, 1963**

By the fall of 1961 Peter and I had been hanging by a thread and we finally went our separate ways. Not long after that, I started going out with a Stanford housemate of my brother's. Andre was a 6' 6" basketball player of French

Me & Andre, San Francisco, 1966
Typical Andre Response

descent, known to be one of the wildest students on campus. He had a motorcycle and we spent many harrowing hours on it. One afternoon after spending Happy Hour at the local beer garden, Andre decided to check in with his fraternity brothers. We rode the bike to the Zete house. When we arrived, he turned to me and said, "hold on tight!" He gunned the engine and we rode up the 20+ steps, through the front door and into the front entrance hall of the Zete house, coming to a screeching stop just in front of a group of his friends. Nothing that Andre did surprised them, though he was asked by the house president not to do it again. How we survived the many post Happy Hour joyrides is a mystery.

Whenever he picked me up on the bike at my parents' house he insisted that my mother go for a spin first. She loved it and was charmed by him. He was very smart though his judgment often didn't affirm it. We had many adventures together during his last two years at Stanford. His Senior Ball was held at a race track in San Mateo, so it could scarcely be called a "Ball," but a lively party celebrating the graduation of those who miraculously made it to the end! From the Ball we went to a nearby party or two and up to San Francisco where we all met at the Tonga Room at the Fairmont Hotel. After numerous rum drinks, Andre stood up, stepped up on the table and dove, fully clothed in his finest (and only) graduation suit, into the pool, definitely not an act the little Polynesian waiters had witnessed before. He climbed out of the shallow end and quickly exited the room out onto the street. We met him there and watched the tourists stare in disbelief as this soaking wet, fully-dressed giant made his way down California Street. The stories of Andre are endless and we were together for four never-a-dull-moment years. We often discussed marriage. I loved him but I knew there would never be the white picket fence with him, nor a secure future. After all, he was French and I knew I would not be the only woman in his life.

In early 1963, Carolan married a man from New York whom she had met in San Francisco. Her wedding was a happy event with a reception at Gammy's house. They stayed in California for a year, until his job in the hotel business took them back to New York. In November of that year Sheila and I took a trip to Tahiti, New Zealand, Australia and the Orient and returned home just before Christmas. I was invited to a Christmas night party at the house of the Countess, Fancy, and the tortoise.

Me & Sheila
Repulse Bay, Outside Hong Kong, 1963

There was a small group of people my age, including the visiting brother of one of our friends. He was a tall (almost 6' 7") very dark-haired young man with movie star looks from New York named Frank Shields. He was as much fun as he was handsome. We hit it off immediately and partied well into the night.

Frank Shields

We were so enamored with one another, by the time we were ready to leave the party, both our rides home had long gone. Frank agreed to walk back with me to my parents' house, which was five miles away. There we were, this gorgeous man in his perfect tuxedo and me in my white off-the-shoulder drapey evening dress, by then barefoot, skipping down the streets of Hillsborough at 2:00 AM on Christmas night. This was the beginning of a cross-country romance that read like a fairy tale. He came from New York every other weekend until he took a job in Downey,

California and then came to San Francisco every weekend. His job there didn't last long and he returned to New York but continued to visit often. He was great fun to be with and fit in well with my friends.

That spring I took him to the Spinsters Ball and when we entered the room, people stopped in their tracks, whispering "WHERE did HE come from?" He had such a huge presence and was so handsome, wherever we went people would stop and do a double-take, but he seemed totally unaffected by the attention. After a few months, he asked me to marry him. Though there was no ring or formal announcement, it was understood between the two of us.

That summer he came out to perform usher duties in a wedding in Carmel. We attended the wedding and all the festivities but something just didn't seem right with him. He had asked me earlier to join him on the red-eye back to New York following the wedding, so I had made plans to take a week's vacation from work to visit my sister and her husband on Long Island. Frank upgraded my coach seat to first-class where we sat together and I felt like royalty. It was very romantic. We arrived in New York, my sister met me at the airport, he kissed me goodbye and said "I'll call you from the office." I waited . . . after five days and no call, I called him and we made plans to have lunch in the City. He told me that something had come up and that it wasn't going to work between us, no details. I was crushed and totally mystified. Seven months later, his daughter, Brooke Shields, was born.

70

San Francisco

I returned to San Francisco where my longtime friend, Lynne, and I sublet a small apartment on Telegraph Hill. I took a job with a PR firm. What an unusual job it was! My boss was Grover Sales, the eccentric acclaimed jazz historian/critic/publicist who had done promotional work for Duke Ellington, Louis Armstrong, Lenny Bruce and other well-known artists. Our clients were, among others, the Trident and the very elegant restaurant, Ondine's, both in Sausalito, the Kingston Trio, the Condor (SF's first topless bar featuring Carol Doda), the Monterey Jazz Festival and various other well-known people and events. One of my assignments was to act as an undercover patron at the Condor, taking mental notes of how customers responded to Carol Doda, the leader of the topless flurry in San Francisco in the early 1960s, reporting on my findings to my boss the following day.

After the PR firm folded, I moved on to work for a talented group of architects, Joseph Esherick & Associates, who at the time were designing The Cannery, a number of BART stations, buildings at UC Berkeley, Sea Ranch and a few private residences. These were amazing people and I was fortunate to have had the opportunity to know and to work for these "high class hippies," as they were named by one of their favorite clients. The only thing about them that would suggest "hippie" was, in spite of their success, they remained totally down-to-earth.

I stayed with them until I was married. While I was working there I was asked to do some amateur modeling for the North Face, a newly-established sporting goods store on Columbus Avenue in North Beach. As I mentioned my aversion to the spotlight earlier, I felt the same way about the camera but decided to take a shot at it. Because their photographer was fun and non-threatening, I adjusted and even learned to enjoy it. Though I wasn't being paid, I was well compensated with the latest in ski outfits and equipment, which worked well for me as we skied every weekend. Coincidentally, this led to a photo shoot for Vogue Magazine, the photos appearing in the "Boutique" section of the March, 1967 issue.

Photo in Vogue Magazine's "Boutique" Section
March 1967

The North Face grand opening included local merchants, restaurateurs, ski enthusiasts, and a motley mix of interesting characters, including a collection of Hell's Angels and a scruffy looking group calling themselves "The Grateful Dead." Few of us had heard of them in those days, but there we were, raising our glasses in celebration right alongside "Pigpen" and the others. Little did we know . . .

**Casual Modeling Picture
San Francisco, 1965**

I recovered from my broken heart and my life began again. My roommate and I moved into a huge flat with my boarding school roommate, Julie. The apartment had room to sleep five comfortably and a living room the length of a bowling alley. I had a date every night, sometimes two in one day, and went sailing, camping or skiing on weekends. Julie eventually moved out to get married and Lynne moved to New York. Word must have gotten around the East coast about this incredible apartment in San Francisco with space available. They arrived in droves, none of whom I'd known previously, friends of friends, a few not my type, a few who were. Roommates came and went as my life went on.

Mike

One of my most loyal supporters was Mike, the host of the party we'd thrown at his parents' house a few years earlier. He was attending law school and living in Berkeley.

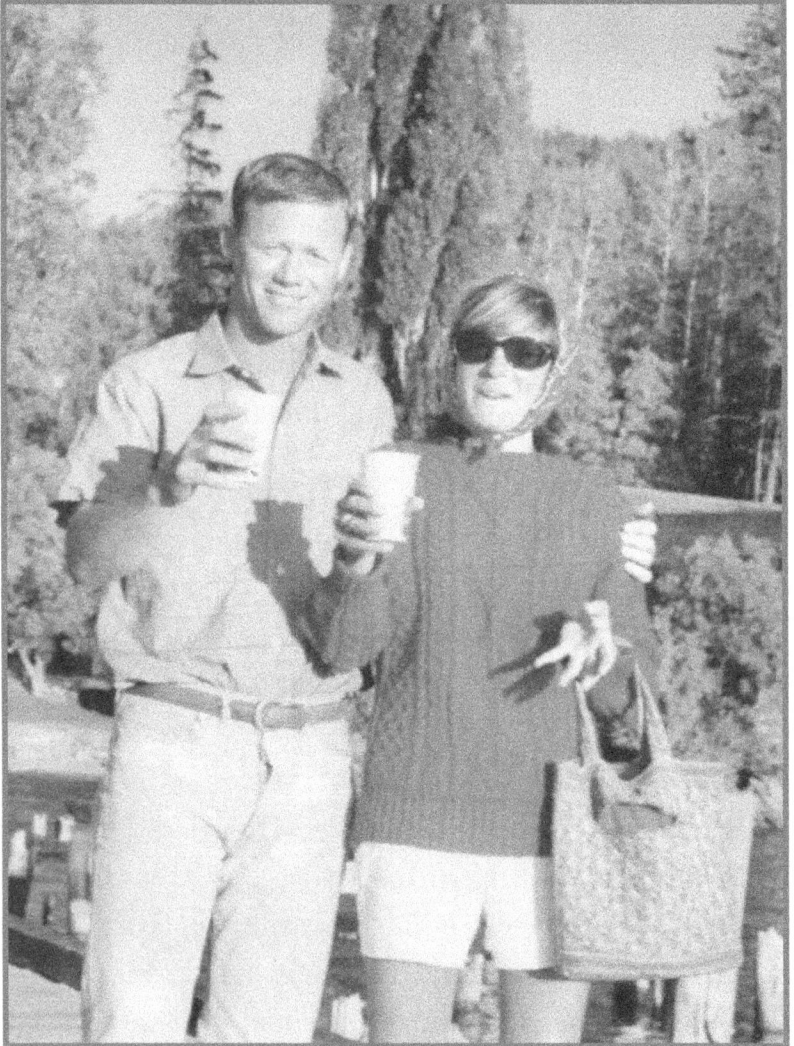

Mike & Me
Tahoe, 1965

Duke, Me & Mike
Virginia Beach, 1967

He was my best friend and he reluctantly accepted the fact that I wanted it to stay that way, just friends. Every Monday he would pick me up at work, take me to my apartment where I'd change my clothes, we'd drop my week's laundry into the machines at the laundromat, head across the Golden Gate to Sausalito to have dinner at the Glad Hand, return to the laundromat, put the clothes in the dryer, and go next door to have a drink until the laundry was done. Now, that's a good friend!

Many weekends we camped at Tahoe in the summer and skied there in the winter. I could rely on him to answer

75

with incredible detail and infinite knowledge any and all political questions I posed. I should have known he would later join Nixon's staff and would become a key adviser to Gerald Ford where he rose to Special Counsel to the President.

Years later, after Eddie and I were divorced, I agreed to meet Mike in Jackson Hole for the 4th of July weekend. He had scheduled a one-day river trip on the Snake River for us with "some friends." His friends turned out to be Dick Cheney, (then Congressman from Wyoming), his wife and two daughters, and Pete McCloskey (then the House Representative from California) and his new wife. We had

Jackson Hole, 1981
(L-R) Mike, Me, Lynn Cheney, Dick Cheney,
Cheney Daughters, Pete McCloskey,
Helen McCloskey, River Guide

a wonderful, relaxed day on the river. Dick Cheney was gentle, easy-going and fun and I often think back on that day and wonder when things changed so dramatically for him. Twenty years later when he was Vice President under George W. Bush, he was rigid, humorless and hawkish— no resemblance to the man I'd met on the Snake River!

Mike and I lost touch for a number of years, but in 1995 when I learned that he had been diagnosed with M.S. I tracked him down. We reconnected and I visited him, his wife and young son in Santa Fe and saw him each time he came to see his mother in San Mateo. We remained in close touch and in 2001, when it became clear that he was not doing well, two of us flew to Santa Fe and visited him in the hospital. He had come to terms with the progression of his illness and seemed to be at peace with it. We laughed over old times, we cried, and we said our goodbyes. He died a few months later.

A group of us flew down for his memorial in Santa Fe where we celebrated his life at a Catholic Mass. The Parish priest officiated, Mike's shaman spoke and his peaceful and devoted Tibetan caretaker comforted all of us. Mike's wife, Jann, had a reception at their house after the service and we met all of their friends, an interesting and eclectic mix. A few weeks later a memorial Mass was held in Burlingame, where his family and California friends came to say goodbye. I was asked in advance to speak a few words. Speaking from the podium in the vast Catholic church was scary, though I did okay. I was thankful to have been followed rather than preceded by letters of condolence and admiration from Dick Cheney, Henry Kissinger, Donald Rumsfeld, Alan Greenspan and Dan Rather!

The Julie Davis Butler Award

Julie and Bill, her college classmate, had been married in San Francisco and moved to Texas where he was in Air Force pilot training. He left for Vietnam in 1966 when they had one child and another on the way. In late 1967 his plane was shot down over Hanoi and he remained a prisoner there for over five years. Julie and some of the other POW wives fought tirelessly for years to get their loved ones released and finally in 1973 Bill came home. Julie was living in San Rafael at the time and the entire city and most of Marin County celebrated his return with a huge parade and day-long festivities. He then attended UC Davis and became a veterinarian. They had another child and moved to a lovely, spacious hilltop house in Calistoga where they continued to raise their children and a curious variety of animals.

When the two older children were grown and the youngest well on her way, Julie went back to work for the same travel agency she'd been with in the 1960s, and in 1987 she took a group she'd known at Stanford to tour the Far East. On the last leg of their trip, while leaving Burma, the plane crashed and all on board were killed. The day I

Julie & Bill, 1984

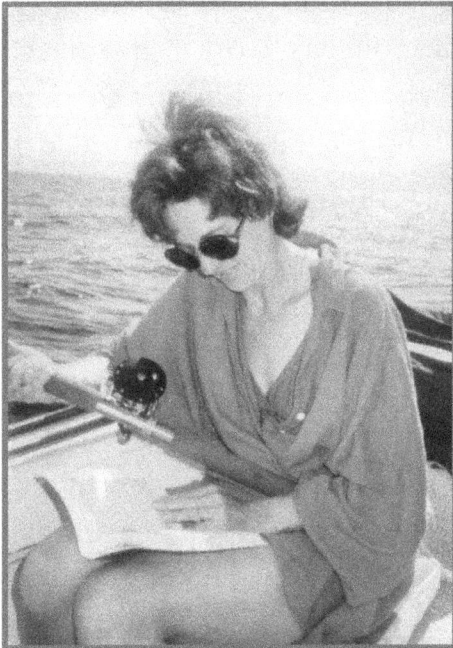

Julie, 1986

got the news was one of the worst days of my life. Today, more than 30 years later, I still miss her terribly, but am grateful to have had those years with her. I learned a lot from Julie. She possessed so many admirable qualities, one being the ability to remain non-judgmental no matter what the circumstances. She accepted me for who I am—an enormous gift to me, as I was no angel.

In the fall after Julie's death, three classmates and I established "The Julie Davis Butler Award," and set up an endowment fund at that time. The plan was to award funds each spring to junior-year students at San Domenico whose proposed projects, to be performed the summer following their junior year, exemplified what Julie stood for. Each year in January the applicants present their projects to our committee and we choose then the ones we feel meet the desired qualifications as works of social justice, peace building, and selfless contributions to humanity and the natural world. The recipients are awarded funds to cover expenses for their proposed projects.

Over the last 30 years the recipients have traveled to Bosnia, China, Vietnam, Ethiopia, Mexico, Chile, Tanzania, and Ireland. They've worked in orphanages, assisted physicians, built houses, taught English and worked for causes in their own neighborhoods. Each September an Assembly is held where each recipient gives a narrated video presentation of her project, her summer's experience, to the student body and visiting alumnae. Since the onset of the JDB Award there have been well over 100 recipients, a fitting tribute to Julie. We are repeatedly honored and impressed by the maturity, dedication and determination of these young women. How times have changed since the carefree summers after our junior year!

Eddie

In November, 1966, I received a call from Eddie Leonard, whom I'd met ten years earlier when he came to California to visit a prep school classmate who was also a friend of mine. Eddie was from the East Coast, and that November had come to Alameda to continue training as a Navy A-6 Intruder pilot. He would leave for Vietnam later that month. He invited me to go out on the "Dependents' Day Cruise" on the USS Enterprise the following Saturday.

Eddie, 1966

What an experience that was! I joined him, some of his fellow pilots, their families and friends on the deck of the massive aircraft carrier. He told me he would be "on duty" for a couple of hours, made sure I was being looked after and said that he would meet me on deck afterwards. The next thing I knew we were being treated to a demonstration on how the jets were flown off and landed on the carrier and he was flying one of them! We stood on a deck above the flight deck and watched them take off, circle around and land. The roar of the engines was deafening and the shaking of the ground (deck) a little unnerving but the excitement of it all was unforgettable. How's THAT for a first date?

That night a group of us went out to dinner after his "show" and we went out every night after that until he left for the Philippines two weeks later. I took him down to meet my parents before he left. We wrote to one another every day, and in March of 1967 I flew to Manila and met him there during his leave. We became engaged there. We traveled around the Philippines and to Hong Kong where we met up with other members of his squadron. Having been there four years earlier I knew about the talented tailors and dressmakers, the bargains and a few great restaurants. We spent a lot of time shopping for silverware and other treasures for our new life together. We had shirts, dresses, suits and shoes made to order, all magically ready within hours.

He returned to San Francisco in early July and we were to be married later that month in Burlingame. After a

Me & Eddie
Hong Kong, 1967

week of parties in our honor, we had a big wedding and a
lively reception at the Burlingame Country Club, left for a
honeymoon in Mexico and New Orleans and moved into
an apartment not far from the Navy base at Virginia Beach.
We returned to San Francisco in November and found a
studio apartment on Telegraph Hill for me to live in while
he completed his second Vietnam tour. He left in January,
and in March I flew to Manila to meet him, this time staying
with a couple I barely knew—Sharon, a childhood friend
of Eddie's whom I'd known briefly through friends in San
Francisco, and her husband, Whitey, whom I'd only met at
their wedding the previous September.

Whitey had taken a job with the Asian Development

Bank in Manila as a speech writer for the bank president, and knowing that Eddie would be taking leave in the Philippines, they had invited me to "come and stay as long as you want." Not knowing them well, I'd anticipated staying maybe a few days before Eddie's leave and a day or so after. Well, we had such a good time together I stayed for six weeks after Eddie returned to duty!

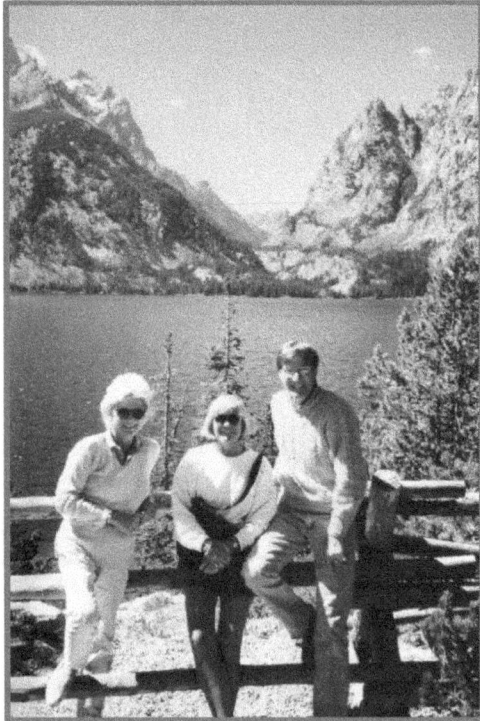

Sharon, Me & Whitey
Jackson Hole, Wyoming, 1996

During those weeks, the three of us were like peas in a pod. I met all of their friends and business associates, went to countless parties with them and learned my way around Manila like a native. They had a driver, a cook, a laundress and a few miscellaneous workers who, combined, cost no more than $100 a week and I never lifted a finger. When it was time to return to San Francisco, I felt as if I was saying goodbye to my family.

LAX Airport, 1982
en route to
Sharon's Surprise 40th Birthday in Cabo San Lucas

Sharon and Whitey returned to New York and eventually settled in Southern California where there was no satisfying Sharon's curiosity or sense of adventure until she landed a job as a Private Investigator with the most notorious PI firm in the LA area. The more scandalous the case, the happier she was. I spent many vacations and many memorable times with them and their family and they treated me like one of them. Unfortunately, after many years of bravely suffering from rheumatoid arthritis and the effects of painkilling drugs, Sharon left us at Christmas of

2011. She is sadly missed by all of us. Whitey and I have stayed in touch and remain close friends.

Eddie, Andrew and Cynthia

In 1968, Eddie returned safely from Vietnam highly honored by the Navy with a number of distinguished medals. But being a war hero at that time carried a stigma to so many Americans, it had to be a very difficult place to be. He never shared how he felt about his experiences, the risks he took, the friends he lost. I'm not sure, even if he had, that I, or anyone, would have understood how he really felt. I was never sure what the U.S. was doing in Vietnam but, without question, I supported him and so many of my good friends, all who were doing what they were ordered to do over there.

We rented a little house in Menlo Park and Eddie entered Stanford Law School in the fall of 1968. I did part-time work for a small architectural firm in Palo Alto until Andrew was born in July of 1970. Eddie graduated with distinction and went to work for a prestigious law firm in San Francisco. We bought a charming ranch-style house in Atherton. Eddie commuted to the city every day and I took well to my domestic role.

Andrew was an easy baby though colic-y during his first few months, at which time the only way to comfort him was to put his infant seat on top of the running clothes dryer. The warmth and vibration would put him to sleep

Cynthia & Andrew, 1973

Cynthia, Me & Andrew, 1976

without fail. As a toddler he entertained himself easily with the help of his imaginary nameless friend. In late 1972 Cynthia arrived and Andrew affectionately named her "Bill." He would proudly introduce her: "This is my sister. Her name is Bill." They were great friends and played together for hours at a time.

Andrew & Cynthia, 1976

I loved being a mom. I did the usual play-groups and kid stuff, and when the children started school, I became involved in their classrooms and the PTA. Eddie worked late hours, played golf every Saturday and spent time with us on Sundays. When he was with the children, he was attentive and affectionate with them and always took time to read to them, even after a long day in the City.

Andrew & Cynthia

We had a fairly active social life on weekend nights thanks to built-in babysitter twins living next door and their parents—"Other Mommy and Other Daddy." We took vacations each summer usually to visit Eddie's family in Southampton, which was exactly as has been described in "W" or Town and Country: every day at the Beach Club, every night at a fancy dinner party, enormous houses, beautiful people. Surprisingly, I was accepted, in spite of my bare feet, and probably because Eddie's family had been there for years and were very well thought of.

Andrew, Me & Cynthia, Cabo San Lucas, 1998

Andrew & Cynthia, Cabo San Lucas, 1998

Sun Valley

Our favorite vacation was visiting my sister and her family in Sun Valley. In July of 1976, I was diagnosed with early stages of cervical cancer. A hysterectomy was recommended and surgery scheduled for early September. In August, the children and I headed for Sun Valley to stay with my sister. Due to Eddie's work schedule, he would follow a week later. During that first week we put together a dinner picnic to include a few out-of-town visitors, some locals and all of our children. We picked a spot that was up a dirt road, along the river, 45 minutes from civilization. We had a lively evening and stayed until the sun went down. After we packed up and prepared to leave, one of the group, a Sun Valley resident whom I had met years earlier at Stanford, a friend of Andre's with a similar *joie de vivre*, asked me to drive back to town with him, which I agreed to do.

He had a bright yellow VW bug convertible, which suited him perfectly. Barely in the passenger seat, with my right foot still outside the car, he backed up. My foot was caught between the running board of the car and a large rock. I remember crying out, "Teddy! My foot!" He stopped the car, jumped out, and seeing my mangled foot, took off his shirt and made a pressure tourniquet to try to stop the bleeding. Luckily, one of the guests had driven a Suburban to the picnic. They threw me in the back of their car and held my foot in the air. Teddy took off in the VW, heading for the hospital as fast as the narrow, bumpy dirt road would allow, to alert the doctors and staff. We followed in the Suburban.

The local doctor met us there and did his best to sew me together. In the meantime, my sister had piled all the kids in her jeep and headed back to Sun Valley. I was ordered to stay in the hospital with my foot elevated for a week. Filled with antibiotics and pain meds, I was not allowed to get out of bed. During that time x-rays were taken and it was determined that my ankle was broken as well, so I had a cast with a window in it so the wound could be monitored for infection. I was being closely watched by the local orthopedic surgeon as well as a renowned Canadian surgeon vacationing in Sun Valley who had been called to observe my condition. I later learned that the doctors were concerned about whether or not I would be able to keep my foot!

By the time I was released from the hospital, Eddie had arrived in Sun Valley. We had a few more days at my sister's before he and I drove back to California. Not much of a vacation for him! My sister kept the children while I entered Stanford Hospital to undergo a hysterectomy. I made history there as the only patient ever to have a hysterectomy with a cast on her leg!

Our visits to Sun Valley were often eventful. In 1979 while there, Eddie played a lot of tennis and was invited to play doubles with George H. W. Bush, who was in the area for a press conference to take place at the Sun Valley Lodge. He had recently completed his position as Director of the CIA and, though we were unaware at the time, was about to go on to bigger and better things. After the tennis match, we offered Mr. Bush a ride to the Lodge in my sister's Toyota Jeep, meant to seat two people comfortably. He took us up on our offer and couldn't have been more easy-going or a better sport as we crammed him and the four of us into the car and drove him to the Lodge where he invited us to attend the press conference. Soon after that, he became Vice President under Ronald Reagan and later was elected 41st President of the United States.

Divorce

A few years after that, our marriage began to crumble. I was needier than I, or anyone, realized and Eddie was, not surprisingly, unable to fulfill my needs. I also realized that I was not cut out to live the country club life (I'd had my fill in my younger years) which was where we were headed. We separated in 1979. We went to therapy together for a few months, which was very difficult and led to the decision to divorce.

Self-examination was painful for me but I stuck with it for many years after we divorced and believe that it, in many ways, saved my life. It was a difficult time for everyone. Eddie moved to the City. He was attentive to the children, taking them on regular weekend outings, and making sure he was there for their Saturday soccer games. After an amicable divorce, we sold the Atherton house. Having had three robberies there (including my diamond engagement ring, which had been in Eddie's family for many years, and numerous valuable pieces from my family), it was a relief to see it go. Andrew, Cynthia and I moved to a nearby cottage in Felton Gables, a safe (or so we thought), desirable area in Menlo Park. And most important, the kids were able to stay in their respective schools—it was familiar territory and they didn't have to make new friends.

Moving On

I established a nice life for myself in Menlo Park. Andrew and Cynthia were busy with school and their friends. After Eddie remarried they often spent weekends with him and Victoria in San Francisco. I had an active social life, and during my 13 years in Menlo Park I had a number of long-term relationships, some of which I look back on and wonder, WHAT was I thinking?

And there were those not-so-long-term experiences, one being with Jeb Magruder, the Nixon aide who spent seven months in prison for committing perjury during a congressional hearing regarding his involvement in the Watergate break-in. I met him a few years after his prison stay and after he, ironically, had been ordained a Presbyterian minister. A few of our dates included my being present at Sunday services where his sermon often told us, the congregation, how to behave "in the eyes of God." I had a hard time believing that he was the right one to be preaching to us. Not surprisingly, our relationship ended abruptly when he showed up 1-1/2 hours late to pick me up for a date with no apology, no explanation. He couldn't understand why I was upset and refused to go out with him ever again.

Somewhere in there, after Andre had survived two divorces, we re-connected, but at (my) arm's length. I often met him and seven or eight of his attorney friends, me being the only female, for Friday lunch at Vanessi's in San Francisco. What a group! They would start with martinis at lunch, then wine, finish up with cognac and then continue through dinner with white powder for dessert and well after. I knew I was unable to keep up with Andre and I didn't try. I think that, thanks to age, Eddie's influence and my being responsible for two children, I no longer felt the need to join him on his wild and crazy adventures. It was not surprising that he became a daredevil race car driver.

Andre, Somewhere in France, 2004

We met for lunch or dinner from time to time and in 2005 he was diagnosed with cancer. When his condition worsened his live-in girlfriend set up a hospital bed in her living room and he received his many friends there. I visited often and in 2006 she threw a birthday party for him, which was also a goodbye party. People came from all over, friends of his I hadn't seen since the 1960s. He was the same old brilliantly witty guy, with his pet dachshund and his 18-month-old granddaughter right there on his bed with him. But it was clear that he was running out of steam. He died on Easter not long after his farewell party. He was another one-of-a-kind. I smile when I think of him; I miss him, his huge presence, his charisma, his intelligence, his contagiously wild imagination, his outrageous wit, his passion and . . . his soft side. Such a unique being. The world just isn't the same without him.

Assault

On the evening of New Year's Day 1985, I had just taken a bath and was relaxing in my bathrobe on my bed watching the last of the Rose Bowl. The kids had spent the week with Eddie and Victoria in San Francisco. I heard a noise in the kitchen, looked up and for a split second I could see the silhouette of a man with a knit cap pulled over his eyes coming at me.

The next thing I knew, he had the pillowcase off my pillow and over my head. He'd obviously had practice. He said, "You have two kids, don't you? Where are they?" I told him they were with their father but would be home any minute. (In truth, they weren't due home for another couple of hours). It was clear he had been watching me and knew my, and my kids' schedules. I asked him calmly if he was going to kill me. He said no, that he was going to rape me.

He did. I fought him as best I could but that was futile and my instincts told me to remain calm. It was over within minutes but before he left through the kitchen door, where he'd entered, he pulled the telephone out of the wall. For reasons I can't explain, seeing the exposed, useless telephone wires was almost as creepy as the assault itself. Unable to call the police from my house, I ran to my neighbor's, an elderly man, the ex-Mayor of Menlo Park. As I stood at the front door, in my bathrobe, calmly describing my ordeal, I caught sight of a nun, his sister, in full habit, sitting at the kitchen table. A scene, the look on her face, so surreal it was almost funny.

The police were called and in less than five minutes four Menlo Park police cars arrived in front of my house. The officers were incredibly kind, compassionate and very gentle. They dusted for fingerprints and gathered whatever evidence they could find. They were required to file a crime report and I calmly told them everything I could remember. I was unable to give a description of the man, but I did remember that he spoke very softly, with a slight southern accent and smelled of soap. Because the responding officers were all male, they called a female officer at home who, kindly, on a holiday, took me to Stanford Hospital, where I underwent an exam, a requirement for all reported rape cases.

By that time, the kids had arrived home with Eddie, and when he saw the police cars and learned why they were there, he took the kids back to San Francisco for the night. (I often wonder how that must have been for them. We never talked about it). After the officers left, a man whom I had dated the previous year came over and took me away to the nicest hotel in the area where I took a warm bath and even slept a few hours, which would not have been possible had I stayed in my house that night.

The next few days and weeks are difficult to describe. The media arrived with their cameras, they interviewed my neighbors, and spread my case all over the local newspapers, though my name was never revealed. It turns out I was the 8th victim in a series of rapes. This man preyed upon blonde, athletic women in their 40s. He was never apprehended but, due to the media attention I received, he never struck again anywhere near Felton Gables.

I received much attention from well-meaning neighbors, support from friends and hundreds of notes from those who I know did not find it easy to express how they really felt about an uncomfortable subject for everyone. With help from a brilliant psychologist provided by the County Victim Assistance Center, I worked through the ordeal and its aftermath. It took some time.

People are often surprised at how open I am about

this ordeal. As I explain to them, it was a life-changing experience but one that resulted in positive changes for me. It brought to the surface a certain strength I never knew I had. It made me realize that my being able to survive this without falling apart, meant I could face just about anything. The experience also revealed who my true friends were. I was disappointed at the lack of support from a few family members and some of my male friends, but I grew to understand that for them it was difficult to accept what had happened to me. They didn't know what to do, so they did nothing. I guess it is also surprising that the assault did not affect my future relationships. It never got in the way. I believe it was a crime of violence, and had no relevance to intimacy.

Andrew

Eddie had always believed that the only legitimate education is an Eastern one, so after much resistance from me, Andrew headed back to St. Paul's in Concord, New Hampshire in September of 1985. I flew back with him, got him settled in his new home-away-from-home and will never forget leaving him there—one of the saddest moments of my life. I remember climbing into my rental car and waving goodbye to him, still a little boy to me. He was about to be swallowed up by the huge stone walls surrounding the centuries-old buildings he would learn to know well.

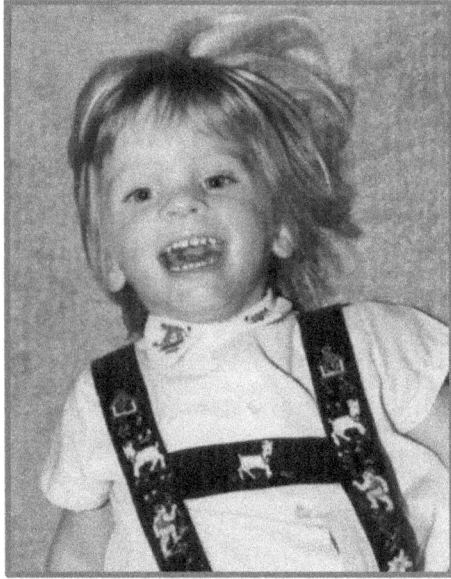

Andrew
1972

Andrew
Graduation from St. Paul's
1989

Andrew & Me
Italy, 1992

I cried the entire way back to California and it took me a long time to adapt to his being so far away. Andrew, after adjusting to the differences in attitude and lifestyles between the West and East coasts, did well. He made some good friends, graduated in 1989 with high honors and received The Rector's Award for "overall excellence and strength of character." At his graduation I remember how stunned I was when they called his name to receive this distinguished award! Of course, as his mother, I was aware of his admirable qualities, but I was so totally moved by the fact that they had been recognized by his teachers and his classmates. I was beyond proud.

He went on to Stanford and has remained in California, presently living in Palo Alto with his wife, Nancy and twin sons, Simon and Thomas. He had been working too many long hours as an investment banker for many years and is presently working for Hewlett-Packard Enterprise, another challenging position. Following suit, Thomas has been attending St. Paul's since last fall and seems to have adjusted well to life on the East Coast. Simon has remained in Palo Alto perfecting his ice skating skills and playing drums in a local band.

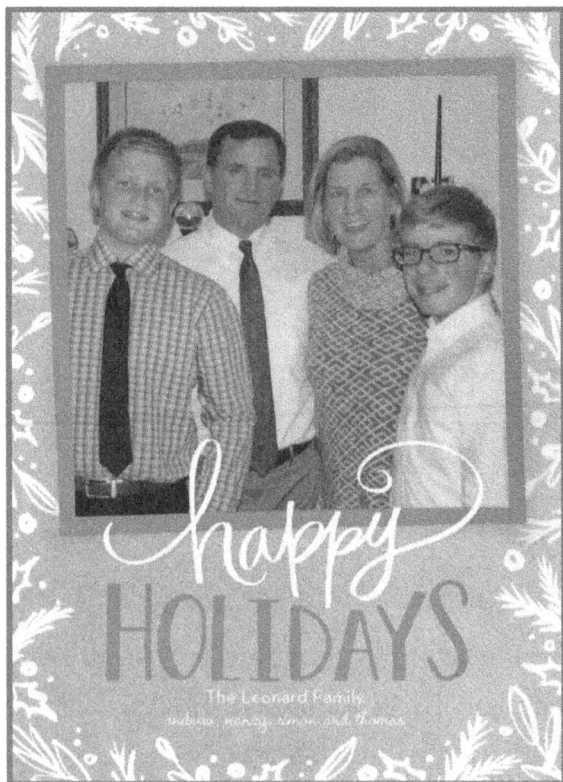

Andrew's Family
Thomas, Andrew, Nancy, Simon

Thomas, Andrew & Simon
Jersey Shore
2006

Thomas, Me & Simon, 2005

Cynthia

After finishing elementary school in Menlo Park, Cynthia attended Crystal Springs Uplands School, a private high school in Hillsborough. Though she complained about it being too small, Crystal Springs was the right place for her. She became a good student and seemed interested in learning. Though, no thanks to my genes, Eddie and I had been blessed with two well-behaved children, Cynthia chose those high school years to sow her oats and gave me a run for my money.

Me & Cynthia
My 60th Birthday

Of course, there weren't many things that she did that I hadn't done myself when I was her age. But she was clever enough to make sure I wasn't aware of everything she did by spending many weekend nights at the houses of her classmates in Hillsborough. I am now aware that our single-level house in Menlo Park, with floor to ceiling easy-to-open windows in her room, made for stealthy escapes.

She graduated from Crystal Springs in 1991 and went to Trinity College in Hartford, Connecticut the following fall. The trip back there to get her settled wasn't as painful for me as the one to St. Paul's had been, as it was clear she was ready to sprout her wings, but it wasn't easy saying goodbye to her either. I visited her there every spring and sat in on some of her classes. I was impressed by each one; the intimacy of the classrooms, the student participation, the candor and interaction with the professors. More than ever I regretted not having taken my own college opportunity more seriously.

Cynthia spent a semester of her junior year in Florence, as Andrew had done two years earlier. I was fortunate to have been able to visit each of them during their months in Italy. After graduation she spent time at various jobs in various places and finally settled in San Francisco. A true city girl, she had a million friends and as many dates. Then she met Mark. After a few years in San Francisco, Mark, being an avid outdoorsman, felt constricted and moved to Bend, Oregon. He'd hoped Cynthia would join him but she wasn't ready to give up the city life.

Finally, in 2003 she decided to give it a try. They were married at Tahoe in 2005 with their devoted Black Lab, Winston, at their side. They live in Bend with their two young boys, Brooks and Logan, and a peppy Black Lab, Woody. Winston left us after a long bout with cancer and I still get teary when I think of him. He and I had a special bond. They've made a great life for themselves and I don't think have ever looked back, though I know that the winters can make San Francisco look pretty good at times.

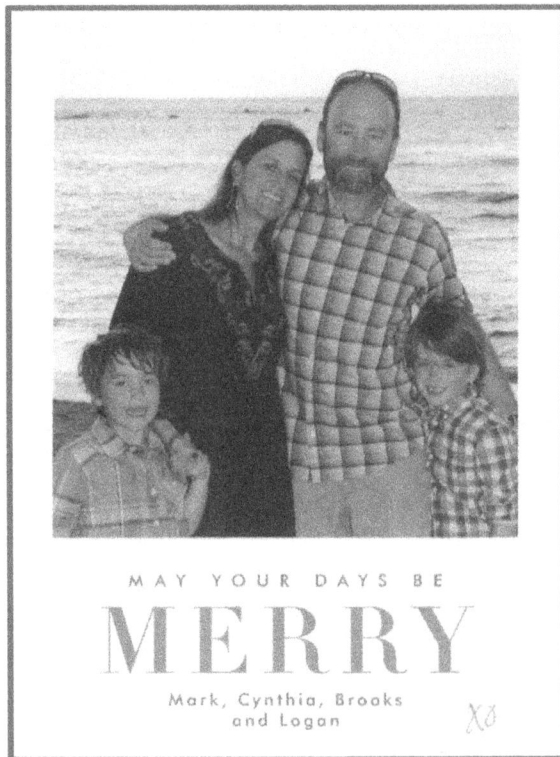

MAY YOUR DAYS BE

MERRY

Mark, Cynthia, Brooks
and Logan

Cynthia's Family
Logan, Cynthia, Mark & Brooks

Back to Work

In 1990 I went to work for an air charter-management company near SFO and adjusted well to the full-time job routine once again. It was an intriguing job, often stressful and frustrating because I was working for a group of ex-Marines who hadn't yet learned that male-chauvinism was no longer "in," and for some corporate pilots who truly lived up to their reputation as prima donnas. But I loved them all. We managed a number of airplanes, some whose owners were men my age whom I'd known back in my single days in San Francisco. I had dated their roommates, partied with them, and who would've guessed back then that these hard-partying, carefree guys would have their own jets 30+ years later and that I would be working for them?

No two days were alike and I learned quickly that the customer is always right. When a man called to inquire about shipping his elephant to Jiddah, I told him I would look into it, which I did and I thrived on the challenge. This request, though bizarre, was not impossible to meet, nor atypical of the charter business, but after hours of research, it was clear that hiring a charter to get the elephant to Jiddah would cost more than the elephant was worth. I suggested he call Fed Ex who will "deliver anything, anywhere, anytime—guaranteed overnight," which they did. The job was never dull!

Willy

In 1992 I began dating a man, whom I'd known in the 1960s, who lived in Tiburon. He was an avid skier, hiker, mountain climber and backpacker. We did a lot of commuting between Marin and Menlo Park and on weekends went backpacking, hiking and skiing. It was difficult for me to juggle it all with a full-time job. Willy was demanding of my time, as he had a lot of free time on his hands. After two years he talked me into quitting my job and moving to Marin. I rented out my house in Menlo Park and we moved into a nice house in Belvedere.

It was a very difficult year. When our lease was up we moved to separate quarters though we continued to see one another. We took some wonderful trips on his Honda Gold-Wing touring motorcycle and those proved to be much more fun than living under the same roof.

Willy & Me
Wind Rivers, Wyoming, 1995

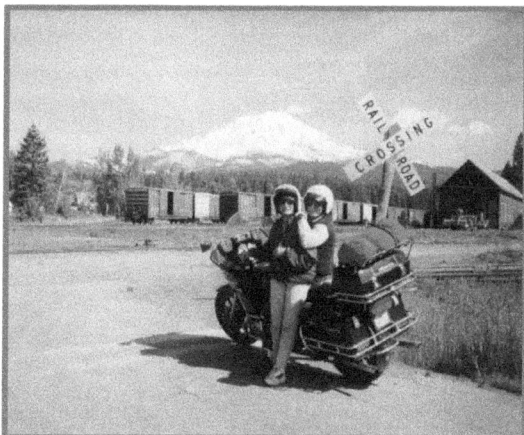

Willy & Me
Shasta, 1995

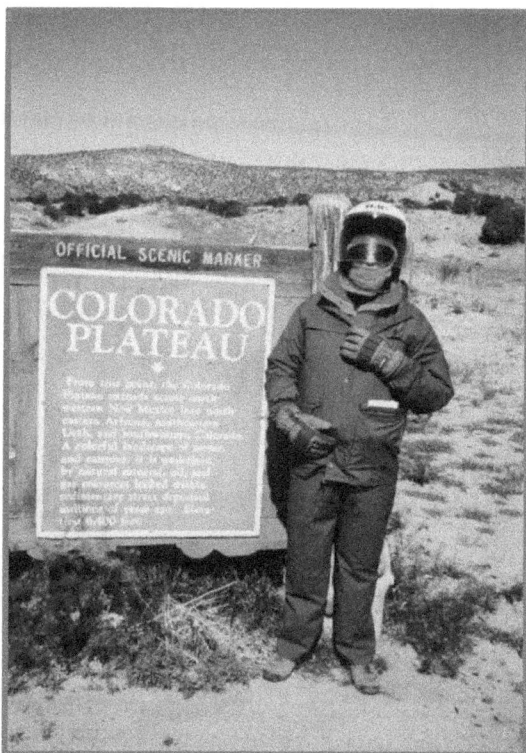

Me, Motorcycle Trip with Willy, 1994
"The Four Corners"
(Utah, Colorado, New Mexico, Arizona)

We covered every inch of the Western States, the San Juan Islands and a few more, met many fascinating people along the way and saw sights we never would have seen otherwise. In 1995 I sold my house in Menlo Park and bought a house on 4th Street in Sausalito. Willy moved to Sun Valley and that was pretty much it for the two of us though we have remained friends.

Sausalito

Moving to Sausalito proved to be a good place to be at the time. Sausalito is a town like no other and I think that "live and let live" was coined there. It's a small town composed of people of all economic levels and political persuasions, some living on boats, others in huge houses, many in-between. It is not a town of ordinary people!

To get the full feel of its diversity, one can get a bird's eye view on Friday evenings during the summer at a free "Jazz by the Bay" concert at Gabrielson Park on the waterfront, a true happening. The entire community shows up and many outsiders as well. Every Friday afternoon I joined a group of regulars there. We were equipped with lawn chairs, a portable fold-up table, gourmet creations/finger foods/hors d'oeuvres/sushi/wine and beer. We often paid little attention to the performances (unless they were terrible, then we noticed!) One of the more unforgettable moments was when I looked up from my place on the lawn to meet eye-to-eye with my

110

gynecologist, a member of the featured jazz group!

I spent some memorable, crazy and funny times with this group. There was always an excuse to get together. We celebrated each of our birthdays, often at Poggio's sidewalk area, with birthday hats, off-color birthday cards, much laughter and always a Carolyn Ford original birthday cake presented to the honoree in a vintage hat box. The other customers, the waiters and those passing by on the sidewalk would undoubtedly want to know what could possibly be so funny. It's quite surprising that Poggio's never asked us to leave. All good, clean fun, but noisy!

Another close-up view of Sausalito's incongruous character could be made by visiting the bocce courts in Dunphy Park on Friday nights in the fall and spring. The first year the "bocce league" was created, I was invited to join a team, with no knowledge of the rules, let alone strategy. Most of us had never played the game but we learned quickly and even won the championship more than once. For some it was very competitive but for me it was more about having a beer with a collection of individuals I never would have met anywhere else (certainly not at the Burlingame Country Club), many of them beyond description.

A day in the life of a true Sausalitan would make an entertaining and colorful sit-com. For the opening scene: an hour at the Nautilus gym, the players being a few smelly boat-dwellers, a disguised retired TV personality, a chatty woman who knows everything and does not allow anyone to use "her" elliptical machine, a couple of well-known Bay

Area news anchors, a retired professor-turned-author, and then just us ordinary residents, all playing their own parts. Some days, there were those of us who could not pretend we'd had a vigorous workout but we certainly did reap the benefits of healthy laughter. The padded area on the floor in the corner of the gym, designed for stretching, is where the truth was often told, some amazing life stories and some of the funniest jokes I've ever heard. I guess there's something about lying on one's back on the floor, next to "real" people, that brings out the best and the worst in each one of us.

Bocce Ball Winning Team!

CASA

After I settled in Sausalito I looked for a project to benefit children—a mentoring situation maybe? In 1996 I was introduced to an organization that piqued my interest: CASA (Court Appointed Special Advocates). Their volunteers are trained to stand in court as advocates for abused and neglected children. I went through the training, which was extensive, intensive and very interesting. The most difficult part of the training was watching a required video about a typically violent case involving a beautiful blond two-year-old boy. The sadness it brought up made me question whether or not I'd be able to handle the job but I went ahead with it, hoping I could make a difference to at least one child.

I learned how widespread child abuse is, how unaware most of us are of its prevalence and I knew then that I needed to do something for the cause. The dedicated staff and the volunteers impressed me as much as the program did and after completing eight weeks of training we were sworn in by a Juvenile Court judge and were assigned individual cases. My first case was a complicated one and lasted for a couple of years. It involved a drug-abusing mother who had two young daughters. She had been in and out of rehab numerous times and was back using when I took the case. I got a full hands-on, unfiltered education in the effects of alcohol and drug abuse, which included my hopeful, not always welcome, visits to the drug rehab centers and half-way houses where she resided, typically situated in the seediest sections of San Francisco.

After much frustration, and her repeated relapses, my case did have a happy ending—the children were adopted by their grandmother. I never heard what happened to their mother. As I was pretty well worn down by that case, my supervisor, who had been very supportive and sympathetic to the challenges of my first case, gently offered me a case that would be less stressful. It was . . . until I had to deal with the father of my "casa" (my assigned subject). He was not at all accepting of my role and he let me know it and did his best to intimidate me. Luckily, his daughter, a very capable, motivated young woman, reached the age of 18 while I worked with her which allowed her to stand up for herself. The people I met while working with CASA were caring, dedicated and supportive and I was sorry to leave them, but after those two stressful experiences I needed to take a break.

Watercolors

During that time, with encouragement from my friend Dinah, an accomplished artist, I took up painting. I had dabbled in it when Andrew and Cynthia were toddlers and always found it therapeutic. Dinah offered me an opportunity I couldn't refuse. I met her at her studio in Napa once a week, and under her supervision, I experimented with printmaking, painting antique furniture and watercolors. Having been raised in a fly-fishing family

114

Watercolor Trout

(my brother was taught to fish at an early age by our French grandmother) I decided to try my luck at painting river trout in watercolor. I continue to work on perfecting my images today. Having had some success in selling them, I have been inspired to keep at it.

The Marine Mammal Center (TMMC)

**"The difference between animals and humans
is that animals change themselves
for the environment, but humans
change the environment for themselves."**

- Ayn Rand

After retiring from CASA, I'd made up my mind to go back to working with animals. As a child, my connection to animals was a special one and that has never changed. For years I had received mailings from the nearby Marine Mammal Center and had always been impressed by their work. In 2002, I looked into their volunteer opportunities, attended the required training classes and signed up for "Tuesday Day Harbor Seals," having no idea what to expect and only a vague idea that there was a difference between an elephant seal, a sea lion and a harbor seal.

I learned on my first day on the job that it was not a place for the weak (physical or emotional) or for one who cared how she looked or smelled! We typically had eight to nine hour days. Some years were more difficult than others, based on the number of pups in our care. There is no better place than the TMMC to witness the animals' reliance on the mercy of Mother Nature and how climate change is affecting their survival. One season the number of harbor

116

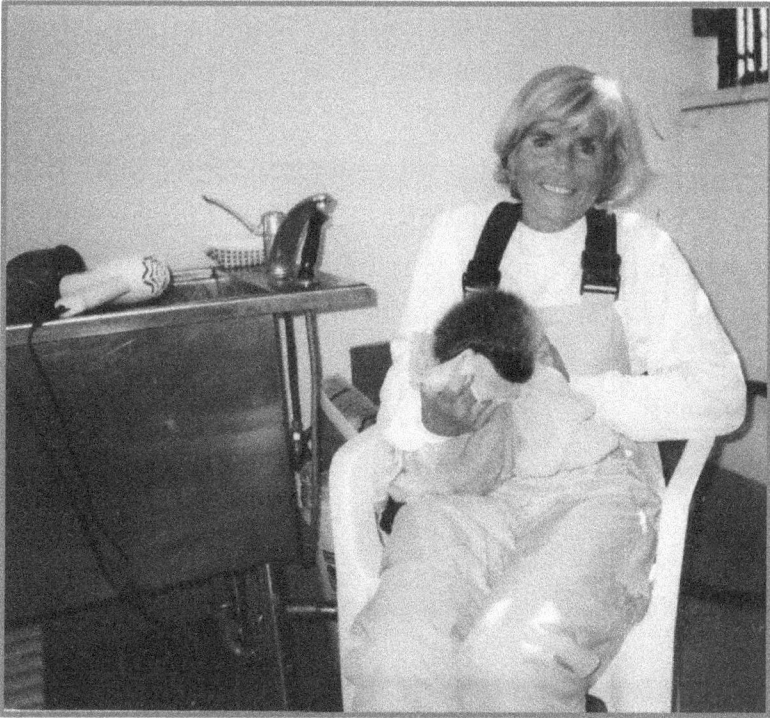

Marine Mammal Center, 2003
Me with "Repo"
Sea Otter in My Lap

seals tripled from the year before, and it became an 11-hour day for me and more than a 14-hour day for some of my crew members who came from significant distances.

I worked in the Harbor Seal Hospital once a week, March through July, for seven years, feeding the pups through syringes and tubes, cleaning their cages and their pools, charting their individual progress and teaching them how to swallow fish. Once we had mastered that and they were able to eat on their own, most of the pups readily gained weight. Then our greatest challenge was getting them on the scale. Lifting 35-40 lbs. of slippery blubber was not an easy feat. We solved the problem by putting each one into a simple plastic laundry basket and weighing the whole load.

After months of rehabilitation, we watched our patients blossom from helpless, emaciated, fuzzy pups into healthy, fat and independent beings, ready to be released back into the ocean where they belong. Watching them go was a satisfying and very emotional experience. I was blessed with a very compatible, experienced crew from the beginning and, though the work was physically challenging, I loved it. I met many caring, committed people at TMMC.

I learned so much about the behavior of these incredible animals. Who would've thought that each one of these adorable creatures would have a personality of his/her own? There were the occasional mellow ones, the stubborn ones, the bratty ones, some who refused to eat, requiring us to force-feed them, and even a rare one who hated the water! I experienced something new each time I entered the Harbor Seal Hospital. Though I no longer volunteer my time at the Mammal Center, I do get together with the friends I met there and have tremendous respect for the work they do there.

Barbie

Throughout my life, there have been many people who've stood out and some who have shaped my life in significant ways. One is a woman named "Barbie." I met her in 1997 when I signed up for the SHARE program at the Marin Humane Society, one of the volunteer groups I joined when I moved to Marin. The purpose of this program is to introduce animals/pets to those in retirement homes, to shut-ins and hospital patients.

The benefits of human interaction with animals are known to be many, one being the alleviation of loneliness. The one drawback in this particular program was that we volunteers were asked to introduce our own animals to the people we were to visit. My cat, Sylvia, whom I'd adopted sight unseen from a vet in Menlo Park, was very shy, not socially adaptable and would never qualify as a cozy companion to a stranger. She trusted only me and my gentle neighbor, Kimberly, and she hated the car. Because cat behavior is never predictable and my situation not unusual, the Humane Society offered "loaners"—dogs, cats, rabbits— who could fill in for our own social flunkies. I assured them that I'd be happy to borrow one, but at the time the only available creature they could offer me was a bantam rooster! I couldn't imagine driving anywhere with a rooster in my car or trying to comfort someone with one, so I declined the offer but told them I'd be happy to do any other assigned task. They asked if I'd be willing to go to San Rafael to feed/walk a dog belonging to "a woman in a wheelchair."

I agreed to give it a try and little did I know what was in store. I walked in the door of this modest house, the smell of fresh baking bread greeting me, and sitting before me was Barbie, a woman a few years younger than I, surrounded by 20+ birds, three cats, and Goldie, her dog. She wore a glorious smile and I felt an immediate warmth I'd rarely felt before. It was as if we'd known one another forever. We talked non-stop, like lifelong friends. I then followed her outside, with Barbie in her wheelchair, and loyal Goldie by her side as we traveled the neighborhood.

At that time, she was in a hand-propelled wheelchair and my only challenge was to keep pace with her and Goldie. Everyone in the neighborhood knew them, and often it would take us an hour to get around the block as they all wanted to stop and chat. At that point she was able, with help, to get out of the chair to slowly stand and move up and down a ramp with parallel bars on both sides that had been set up in her living room, and was able to get to the bathroom with help. My visits became a weekly event and each time I went to her house I would meet a different San Rafael fireman coming or going. Barbie had six bread machines placed around the living room. I would help her mix the ingredients, she would pour the batter into the machines, press the buttons and 40 minutes later, *voila!*— six loaves lovingly baked for the firemen. They would always arrive in one fire engine or another so I knew not to be alarmed if there was a big red fire engine parked outside her house when I arrived. They were gladly willing to help her in or out of her wheelchair, onto the parallel bar ramp and were at times called in to pick her up off the floor. But she refused to give up!

As time passed, her condition worsened, she had to give up the bread-making, was no longer able to stand and was fitted for an electric wheelchair. Though she became more dependent upon me, I loved being with her and her beloved animals and we had some very funny moments together, but it was becoming clear that I couldn't fulfill her needs alone. I decided to introduce my dear friend, Karen, to Barbie. Karen had recently lost her husband to a brain tumor and I thought she would never recover. I had tried everything to help alleviate her grief and thought that maybe meeting this incredible woman would at least temporarily take her mind off her loss.

It worked. From then on we went to Barbie's as a pair every Friday to do whatever needed to be done—paying Barbie's bills, doing her laundry, cleaning the bird cages, exercising Goldie, rescuing her cat from the attic, feeding her lunch. We in turn were rewarded in spades just by being with her. Oftentimes, on a warm sunny day we would head outside to her backyard, Barbie leading the way with her pet cockatoo, Oliver, on her shoulder, Goldie following close behind and at least one cat following him. Among our many funny experiences at Barbie's was a run-in with a visiting rabbit that Barbie was keeping temporarily for a friend. He escaped his cage and had Karen and me chasing after him, tripping over him as he ran between our legs, taking full advantage of his newfound freedom. This went on for an hour and he was loving every minute of it, not to mention Barbie. She was in hysterics, tears running down her cheeks, watching these two over 60-year-olds being outsmarted by a bratty little bunny!

We did finally succeed in capturing the little devil. By

that time Barbie had lost control of her muscles and was able to move her wheelchair and answer her phone by moving her head. She remained beautiful and vibrant with never a complaint. She assured us, saying "I am the luckiest person in the world to have all these fabulous people around me." And I think she sincerely believed it. She had a constant stream of visitors throughout the day who did what they could to make her comfortable. Unfortunately, her little body finally gave out in October 2017. She was like a ray of sunshine, a gift to all of us. Barbie taught me more about what's really important in life than anyone I've ever known. And 20 years ago I thought I was just going to feed a woman's dog . . .

Dream Cottage

The weather in Sausalito is as varied as are the residents, with seven different climates within the Sausalito city limits. My house on 4th Street was in the heart of "Hurricane Gulch." It was a beautiful house with a stunning view of the Bay Bridge and some of San Francisco. After 13 years, when I had had enough wind, fog and freezing temperatures and too many maintenance problems, I sold the house in 2008 and moved to a partially-restored cottage in an area called "The Banana Belt." I had gone from a view of the water, the Bay Bridge, to an area tucked away against a hill, with no water in sight.

I had been looking forward to the warmer climate,

but before long I realized that this so-called banana belt had to be a real estate agents' marketing term. My dream cottage, located creekside, shaded by hundreds of trees and up against a hillside, was damp and cold. It didn't take much for me to realize I'd made a huge mistake. I had always wanted to live in a cottage. This was the perfect find, I thought: charming, yellow with white trim and, even better, had been partially remodeled with recycled countertops, bamboo floors, fuel-efficient appliances. I was duped, being the environmentally-conscious person I'd grown to be.

It turned out that the house had numerous problems due to the dampness, none of which had been disclosed when I bought it. Two years after the move I received a summons from the buyer of 4th Street alleging that she had discovered more dry-rot damage, (I had spent thousands repairing dry-rot damage at the time of the sale) that she claimed I/my contractor had tried to cover up. The work I'd had done had passed all inspections, all contingencies had been lifted at the time of the sale, so her claim caught me totally off guard. I, never having had to defend myself in court before, appeared in front of the judge to find myself up against the owner, a seasoned CEO accustomed to speaking in public, with all the correct legal lingo, and her case file perfectly flagged by "Exhibit #1, Exhibit #2," etc. I barely knew what an exhibit was. I stuttered and stammered through my testimony but I guess the judge knew that I was telling the truth. I won the case.

Six months later, during a heavy rainfall, I

experienced a flash flood, due to a clogged city-maintained storm drain at the hill above my house. Tons of water, a true waterfall, rushed down the hill into my yard and my house. Afraid to stay in the house, I went out to wait for the fire department to arrive, and if I hadn't held onto a nearby parked car, I would have been swept down the street, the water was so forceful. It was a nightmare, very scary and it took weeks to dry everything out. The lower level never did recover. I was forced to take the City of Sausalito to court to recover my losses. The flooding was the result of negligence on their part as this storm and its possible dire consequences had been predicted for days, with plenty of warning to clear the storm drains.

Having to go back to court again within a year for a house-related issue was almost more than I could handle. Though I won this case too, having to take anyone to court, let alone City officials, was so against my grain, I put the house on the market. It became clear to me that owning a house in Sausalito was not for me.

Sonoma

After 17 years in Sausalito, I moved to a quiet rental in a cul-de-sac near the western Sonoma hills, not far from the historic Plaza, but far enough away to avoid the weekend tourists and wine tasters. It is quiet and warm in the summer, my doors and windows stay open at night, the sound of crickets lulling me to sleep—a far cry from the days and nights I froze in Sausalito. Though I haven't missed the fog, the traffic or the Sausalito politics for a minute, I think back on my many good times there, and I do occasionally miss the craziness and the close proximity to my friends there, but they make frequent visits to Sonoma and I spend time with them in Sausalito as well. We still celebrate birthdays together whether it be in Sonoma or Sausalito.

I'm enjoying the easy pace and am forever grateful to be free from the stress of owning a house. Though it took two years to establish some good friendships here, I've met some wonderful people, have become involved in some local causes and I feel very much included. I make an effort to go to the gym every day, as I did in Sausalito, and even ride a stationary bike, often referred to as "Jeanne's bike," where I pedal away, listening to others' stories, as they do mine. Many of the people I've met at the gym have become close friends.

Sonoma is a warm and giving community. The wildfires of October 2017 showed the world how a small town can survive, thanks to caring people coming together to help friends, feed neighbors, take in strangers. There are still, eight months later, hand-painted signs dotting the roads thanking the first responders, firefighters, volunteers for saving our town. I was one of the lucky ones. Due to mild smoke damage in my house, I was displaced for only 11 days. So many lost everything they owned. The devastation is still evident and we're still feeling the effects, but the rebuilding is proceeding and wildflowers and brilliant new growth are visible everywhere.

In looking back on my 70+ years, the many experiences I've retold (and those I've excluded, for my own preservation) have all had a touch of humor somewhere and I believe that that has been a gift that was carved out way back at 250 Roblar. Without humor, I'm not sure I would have made it through some of my most trying times. I know that I wouldn't have made it without the support from my family and my amazing friends. Beginning in childhood, I've always had a number of cherished friends. And since I've been single, I've been blessed with friends who have been like family to me. I've been included in birthdays in Hawaii, Cabo, Santa Barbara and San Diego, family celebrations in faraway places, weddings in New York, San Diego, Seattle, gatherings in Palm Desert, visits to Puerto Vallarta, summers at Fallen Leaf Lake. In all these places and in their houses, there is always a guest room waiting for me.

I could go on for many pages about my friends, their generosity, their accomplishments, but more important, how they've offered their support, emotional and otherwise. There are those with whom I can share my innermost thoughts, feelings and concerns, never feeling judged. I am so fortunate and am forever grateful to have them in my life. They all have remarkable stories of their own to tell but I will leave that up to them.

As Maya Angelou has said, "I've learned that sometimes life gives you a second chance." While writing my story, so many of my life's "second chances" have

My Birthday, 1986

come to mind. A few I have mentioned, many I have not. I believe there is "someone" watching over me—it is the only explanation for my having survived these close calls relatively unscathed. I've been given too many second chances to disregard them as mere coincidences.

Acknowledgments

Thank you to Karen Mireau Rimmer at Azalea Art Press for encouraging me to turn my unpolished draft into something readable. I refer to Karen, a petite, efficient, affable woman, as my "publishing team." She skillfully guided me to the finish line without judgment, reassuring me whenever I doubted myself or my ideas. I am forever grateful to her for her support and her expertise, but more for her friendship.

I've learned
that people will forget what you said,
people will forget what you did,
but people will never forget
how you made them feel.

- Maya Angelou

To Contact the Author
please email
jgpleonard@gmail.com

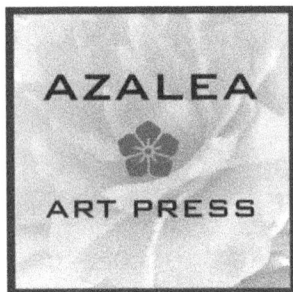

AZALEA

ART PRESS

To Contact the Publisher
please email
Azalea.Art.Press@gmail.com

www.ingramcontent.com/pod-product-compliance
Lightning Source LLC
Chambersburg PA
CBHW021011090426
42738CB00007B/744